Welcome Home, C

A version of *Le Voyageur sans bagage* by
Jean Anouilh

Jean Anouilh (1910–87), French playwright born in
Bordeaux, made his name in France with *Le Voyageur
sans bagage*. His popularity spread to the English-
speaking world in the post-war period with the success of
Antigone. He categorised his plays as *pièces roses* (*Time
Remembered, Dinner with the Family*), *pièces noires*
(*Eurydice, Antigone, Medea, Romeo and Jeanette*), *pièces
brillantes* (*Ring Round the Moon*), *pièces grinçantes*
(*Ardèle, Waltz of the Toreadors*) and *pièces costumes*
(*Becket, The Lark*).

Anthony Weigh is a graduate of the Masters in Playwriting
programme at the University of Birmingham. His first
play, *2,000 Feet Away*, had its world premiere at Belvoir
Theatre, Sydney, in 2007 and its UK premiere in 2008
at the Bush Theatre, London, directed by Josie Rourke,
as was *Like a Fishbone* in 2010. His version of Lorca's
Yerma was staged at the Gate Theatre in 2011 and his
adaptation of the Vercors novella *The Silence of the Sea*
by the Donmar Warehouse in 2013. Other plays include
Broad Street, or How Do I Strike You? (University of
Birmingham), *The Flooded Grave* (Bush Theatre, London)
and *The Middle Man* (Bush Theatre, London). His new
play, *Edward II*, will premiere at Malthouse Theatre,
Melbourne, in July 2016. He was Playwright in Residence
at the National Theatre in 2009, has been Associate
Playwright at the Bush Theatre and is a former Associate
Artist of the Donmar Warehouse.

ANTHONY WEIGH

Welcome Home, Captain Fox!

a version of *Le Voyageur sans bagage* by
JEAN ANOUILH

FABER & FABER

First published in 2016
by Faber and Faber Limited
74–77 Great Russell Street, London WC1B 3DA

Jean Anouilh, *Le Voyageur sans bagage*
© Éditions de La Table Ronde, 1958

Typeset by Country Setting, Kingsdown, Kent CT14 8ES
Printed in England by CPI Group (UK) Ltd, Croydon CR0 4YY

A CIP record for this book is available from the British Library

ISBN 978-0-571-33141-6

2 4 6 8 10 9 7 5 3 1

To Karen
with thanks

Introduction

In the early hours of 1 February 1918 a train pulled into a railway siding in Lyon. It was carrying French troops being repatriated from German prisoner-of-war camps. Gradually the train disgorged its hollow-faced passengers and the station emptied to the sounds of reunited families eager to catch up on the lost years.

It was then that a figure was seen wandering aimlessly along the platform. A solider. Lost. When asked his name he answered, 'Anthelme Mangin'. Other than that he had no memory of who he was, or of what had happened to him prior to arriving on a Lyonnaise railway platform on a frigid February night.

Among those enthralled by Mangin's story was the young playwright Jean Anouilh, who was searching for a subject for one of his early plays. To him there was something poignant and funny about the way in which Mangin was hawked around from family to family by psychiatrists in an attempt to discover his true identity, and in 1937 Anouilh's comedy, *Le Voyageur sans bagage*, fictionalising one such meeting, opened in Paris to critical acclaim.

As I began to think about reimagining Anouilh's play for a new adaptation at the Donmar Warehouse in London, Artistic Director Josie Rourke mentioned the long tradition in French literature of the unknown man, often a soldier, walking out of a dim past without class or station to make life anew. A character like Dumas' Martin Guerre or Hugo's Jean Valjean.

7

It occurred to us that there was another culture just as fascinated by tales of the unknown man. America. From Jay Gatsby to Don Draper in the television series *Mad Men,* American culture was littered with history-less men, remaking themselves with stories about who and what they were. Those stories were their currency.

This spoke to me of the questing, self-dramatising world of America of the 1950s. While Europe was struggling out from under years of war and conflict, America was glowing with affluence and optimism. Deliriously capitalistic, the returned veteran and his young family might settle down each evening in front of a spanking new TV set to watch the latest episode of *I Love Lucy* while eating freshly thawed TV dinners out of newly purchased refrigerators. It was a world that was perfectly captured in the sumptuous filmed melodramas of Douglas Sirk and the glittering comedies of Billy Wilder.

As I sat down to gladly binge my way through these masterpieces of the American cinema – *The Apartment, Some Like It Hot, Imitation of Life* – I began to think about the act of adaptation. To me adaptation is a conversation. A conversation between the original author and the adapter. Sometimes it's a pretty polite affair. Sometimes it needs to be a bit more verbose. Boisterous even. I wondered if the conversation I was having with Monsieur Anouilh might benefit if I invited a few more guests to the party. I wondered if by taking the broad dramatic arc of Anouilh's original play, and reflecting it through the set of circumstances provided by my new pals Sirk and Wilder and their version of America in the 1950s, something new and delighting might not turn up.

So, I took Anouilh's lost man, gave him a nice short haircut, bought him a smart Brooks Brothers suit, introduced him to the kind of Martini-soaked family that would have made even Freud's eyes water, handed him a gun and plunged him in. Shaken and stirred. Hopefully the result is a tasty cocktail of identity lost and found and lost again. A very human and forgiving story about a man with no memory found wandering along a railroad track, desperate for happiness, whose future is only as bright as the story he chooses to tell about his past.

ANTHONY WEIGH

Welcome Home, Captain Fox! was first performed at the Donmar Warehouse, London, on 18 February 2016. The cast, in alphabetical order, was as follows:

Juliette Michelle Asante
George Fox Barnaby Kay
Gene Rory Keenan
Mrs Marcee Dupont-Dufort Katherine Kingsley
James Trevor Laird
Mrs Fox Sian Thomas
Mr De Wit Depont-Dufort Danny Webb
Valerie Fenella Woolgar
Man in a White Coat / Uncle Job Daniel York
with
Kit Connor
Ilan Galkoff
Rory Stroud

Director Blanche McIntyre
Designer Mark Thompson
Lighting Designer Hugh Vanstone
Sound Designer Gregory Clarke
Casting Director Alastair Coomer CDG

Characters

in order of appearance

Gene
late thirties to early forties

Man in a White Coat
forties

Mrs Marcee Dupont-Dufort
she'd never tell

Mr De Wit Dupont-Dufort
older than Marcee

James
the oldest

Mrs Fox
late sixties

George Fox
late forties

Valerie Fox
late thirties to early forties

Juliette
early thirties

Small Boy
ten-ish

Uncle Job
forties

WELCOME HOME, CAPTAIN FOX!

Prologue

Click.
  Harsh light.

Gene Tuna fish.

Man in a White Coat Breakfast?

Gene Boiled ham.

Man in a White Coat Supper?

Gene Meatloaf.

Man in a White Coat Thursday?

Gene Food?

Man in a White Coat Anything.

Gene Movie night?

Man in a White Coat What'd ya see?

Gene Marilyn. Jack Lemmon. Tony . . . What's his? They get dressed up as –

Man in a White Coat Fruits! Week before?

Gene *Invasion of the* – Whatchamacallits.

Man in a White Coat Piece o' crap.

Gene You a critic?

Man in a White Coat Cute. January then?

Gene Movies?

Man in a White Coat Current events.

Gene Cuba? Castro?

Man in a White Coat Like Castro, do you?

Gene Wait! Alaska.

Man in a White Coat Whadaboutit?

Gene Became the forty-ninth state.

Man in a White Coat Sure?

Gene Yes. No. Wait! Yes. Hawaii this August makes fifty.

Man in a White Coat President?

Gene Eisenhower.

Man in a White Coat Vice?

Gene A character flaw.

Man in a White Coat President!

Gene Nixon. I'm kidding.

Man in a White Coat Funny. Sputnik?

Gene Space rocket.

Man in a White Coat Like commie rockets, do you?

Gene Not particularly.

Man in a White Coat See many of them in Russia, did you?

Gene It was Germany.

Man in a White Coat Near enough. How's about school?

Gene In Germany?

Man in a White Coat Germany? Russia? You tell me, comrade.

Gene I'm pretty sure I'm not from –

Man in a White Coat Where'd you go to school then?

Gene I don't –

Man in a White Coat Play sports?

Gene Did I?

Man in a White Coat Baseball? Football? Swim team? You on the swim team? How's about a pet?

Gene A pet?!

Man in a White Coat A family pet? Growing up?

Gene Maybe.

Man in a White Coat Dog, was it?

Gene I –

Man in a White Coat Cat? More of a cat man, are ya?

Gene Cats! I'm not sure I –

Man in a White Coat Favourite food?

Gene Food?

Man in a White Coat Growing up in – Where'd you grow up in again?

Gene I'm trying to –

Man in a White Coat Bananas?

Gene Bananas?

Man in a White Coat Cornflakes? Ketchup? Rutabagas?

Gene Rutabagas?

Man in a White Coat As a kid in – where'd you say that was again?

Gene I don't think –

Man in a White Coat Mac and cheese? Waffles? Pretzels? How's about Cheesy Puffs?

Gene Cheesy Puffs?

Man in a White Coat You gotta like Cheesy Puffs. Every kid likes Cheesy Puffs.

Gene Do I? Do they?

Man in a White Coat Of course they do . . .

Man in a White Coat They're cheese for Christ's sake! They're cheese. And they puff. What's not to like? What's not to like about Cheesy Puffs? Everybody likes –	**Gene** If you give me a – I'm trying to – Do I like Cheesy Puffs? Wait! I think – Maybe – Wait, gimme a – Dammit! I don't know! I don't know! *I DON'T KNOW!*

Gene slams his fist down on the desk in exasperation. The phone buzzes. The Man in the White Coat picks it up. Listens. Replaces the receiver. Sits back in his chair and takes a drag on his cigarette through yellowed fingers. Gene sits with his head in his hands.

Man in a White Coat Let's go back to lunch then.

Gene Lunch?

Man in a White Coat Yeah. What'd you have for lunch?

Gene *(defeated)* Tuna fish.

Man in a White Coat Breakfast?

Gene Boiled ham.

Man in a White Coat Supper?

Gene Meatloaf.

Black.
And Charles Trénet sings . . . 'Boum!'

One

*The living room of a grand shingled estate house
somewhere on the South Fork of Long Island. Rooms
of this kind are never nearly as large as you've imagined
them to be. These houses are merely holiday homes –
albeit holiday homes for folks who take a lot of long
holidays. In the distance Charles Trénet sings 'Boum!' on
a record player. It echoes through the empty rooms like
he's singing with his head stuck in a cast iron bedpan.*

*Mrs Marcee Dupont-Dufort stands looking out of a
large window to a terrace and, beyond that, to the
swimming pool and, beyond that, to the lawn and,
beyond that, to the dunes and, beyond that, to the sea
which winks at us from time to time in the midday heat.*

*Mr De Wit Dupont-Dufort is curled up on himself in
some corner or other. Hiding behind a golfing magazine,
no doubt. Anyway, to begin with we don't see him, as he
really doesn't want to be seen.*

Marcee Dupont-Dufort What are you? You strange,
strange thing. Just standing there. Gazing into the
swimming pool, like a – like a – What? Like some kinda
animal. Like some kinda wild animal or something. A
deer or a gazelle or – an elk! That's it! An elk! By a pond.
Gazing at its reflection. Waiting. Listening. Ready to
make a run for it. (*Darkening.*) You better not. You hear
me? You better not make a goddamned – (*Getting an
idea! Suddenly brightening.*) You know what it's like?
You're like? An alien. An alien being. Sent here in the
nick of time just before his home planet gets vaporised
by nukes or something. Sent here as a baby in a teeny
tiny spaceship. Whizzing past what'sits – galaxies or

something, and landing smack bang in the middle of – I don't know. Ohio or something. One of those Ohioy kinda states. The flat ones, anyway. In the middle. And he gets discovered by a nice homey couple. Farmers. And they take him home. Adopt him kinda. And then one day. Years later. He comes to them. The farmy couple. The little adoptive farmy couple from Ohio. And he says. He says: 'Mom? Pop?' And they say: 'What, son?' And he says: 'I gotta go find out who I really am.' And she – the mom. She cries. And the father asks him if he's sure. And he says he's sure. And they shake hands nice and firm. And the son. The alien son heads off into the –

De Wit Dupont-Dufort It's Superman.

Marcee Dupont-Dufort I'm saying something.

De Wit Dupont-Dufort Yeah, it's Superman.

Marcee Dupont-Dufort I'm telling you something.

De Wit Dupont-Dufort Yeah, you're telling me Superman.

Marcee Dupont-Dufort What if I am?

De Wit Dupont-Dufort Superman's a comic.

Marcee Dupont-Dufort *Like* Superman is what I'm saying.

De Wit Dupont-Dufort He doesn't *look* like Superman.

Marcee Dupont-Dufort I'm talking in what'sits.

De Wit Dupont-Dufort Nonsense?

Marcee Dupont-Dufort Metaphors.

De Wit Dupont-Dufort He lives in a nut-house.

Marcee Dupont-Dufort For now.

De Wit Dupont-Dufort Superman doesn't live in a nut-house.

Marcee Dupont-Dufort You heard of metaphors?

De Wit Dupont-Dufort If you're going to go using metaphors, Marcee, you might as well get it right.

Marcee Dupont-Dufort An alien is what I'm saying.

De Wit Dupont-Dufort You been watching too much TV.

Marcee Dupont-Dufort I'm kidding around.

De Wit Dupont-Dufort (*referring to her mental state*) Your roof is leaking.

Marcee Dupont-Dufort Ever heard of that, De Wit? Kidding around?

De Wit Dupont-Dufort I can kid around. I can kid around plenty. I can kid around plenty when I don't have to get up at the break o' dawn and drive out to Picatinny, New Jersey, to pick up some cracked-up chump from a US Navy nut-house and ferry him a hundred and fifty miles in the opposite direction to the end of Long Island so we can find out if these *Hampton* types are the crack-ups family or not, in a hundred degrees!

Marcee Dupont-Dufort Keep your voice down.

De Wit has taken out a cigar.

And don't smoke those in here.

De Wit Dupont-Dufort Why not?

Marcee Dupont-Dufort It's not that kinda place.

De Wit Dupont-Dufort How do you know?

Marcee Dupont-Dufort I can just tell.

De Wit Dupont-Dufort Really?

Marcee Dupont-Dufort Yeah. 'Really'.

De Wit Dupont-Dufort Cos it looks kinda shabby to me.

Marcee Dupont-Dufort Some people have so much class they don't have to try.

De Wit Dupont-Dufort Then these people must have a ton o' class.

Marcee Dupont-Dufort What am I talking *class* to you for?

De Wit Dupont-Dufort I'm missing my Rotary meeting to be talked at like this?

Marcee Dupont-Dufort Rotary will still be there when we get back.

De Wit Dupont-Dufort Not by the time we drive that crack-up back out to Picatinny, New Jersey, and get back into the city and –

Marcee Dupont-Dufort For a start, he won't be going back to Picatinny, New Jersey. He's going to be staying right here, if he knows what's good for him. And secondly, there's always Rotary next week. Rotary meets every week, De Wit. Every week on a Thursday night. Every week on a Thursday night in that tacky restaurant downstairs at the Roses Club.

De Wit Dupont-Dufort I thought you liked the Roses Club.

Marcee Dupont-Dufort The Roses Club is OK as far as alligator clubs go, but it isn't the Harvard Club and it sure isn't the Waldorf.

De Wit Dupont-Dufort You've just gotta thing against Linda Glass.

Marcee Dupont-Dufort I do not have a thing against Linda Glass.

De Wit Dupont-Dufort You do so have a thing against Linda Glass. Ever since she handed you her coat that night in the lobby of the Roses Club.

Marcee Dupont-Dufort She was making a point.

De Wit Dupont-Dufort It was an honest mistake.

Marcee Dupont-Dufort She was making a point.

De Wit Dupont-Dufort She thought you were the coat check girl.

Marcee Dupont-Dufort She was making a goddamned point!

De Wit Dupont-Dufort And the point was you looked like the goddamned coat check girl! You were in that hat!

Marcee Dupont-Dufort 'That hat' cost me fifteen dollars.

De Wit Dupont-Dufort 'That hat' cost *me* fifteen dollars.

Marcee Dupont-Dufort Everyone's wearing hats like that this year.

De Wit Dupont-Dufort Everyone who works as a coat check girl.

Marcee Dupont-Dufort If Linda Glass had half a brain she'd know that everyone's wearing hats like that this year.

De Wit Dupont-Dufort *If* you're a coat check girl.

Marcee Dupont-Dufort Linda Glass was making a point is what she was doing. Linda Glass was making a point about us coming from Miami Beach and you having to *make* your money and not get it handed to you on a silver what'sit, and how we don't spend summers out here in Amagansett or wherever but schlep to that awful run-down holiday club in the Catskills . . .

De Wit Dupont-Dufort I thought you liked the Catskills! It's gotta lake! You like the Bergsteins – Glovchicks? She sat nice with you and talked all day that day you got impetigo from swimming in that pool, like I told you not to. Frankly people don't think your breasts are half as interesting as you do. That's including me by the way. Did you hear what I said?

Marcee Dupont-Dufort . . . Full of people like the Bergsteins and the Eddelmans and the Glovchicks and the Harrimans – Martha Glovchick kept fondling my breasts. She kept saying I had something on my blouse and finding reasons to wipe me with her handkerchief. Wiping my breast. Pressing her handkerchief right up against my breast. She's so *Jewy!*

James comes in.

James The Foxes say they'll be right along. In the meantime is there anything I can get for you folks?

Marcee Dupont-Dufort No. No, thank you. No we're – We're just fine. Thank you. Thanks a lot. Thanks.

James What about the . . .

Marcee Dupont-Dufort The . . .

De Wit Dupont-Dufort The crack-up. He means the crack-up.

Marcee Dupont-Dufort The . . . Oh, well you could go ask him I guess. He's out by the swimming pool.

James I'll go ask him then.

Marcee Dupont-Dufort Yes. Yes, why don't you do that?

De Wit Dupont-Dufort Careful. He bites.

Marcee Dupont-Dufort (*through clenched teeth*) De Wit!

James They'll be right along.

He goes.

Marcee Dupont-Dufort That man makes me indescribably happy.

De Wit Dupont-Dufort Who? The . . .

Marcee Dupont-Dufort 'They'll be right along.' 'They'll be right along.' There's something, isn't there? About a good butler.

De Wit Dupont-Dufort We got a butler.

Marcee Dupont-Dufort Ha! Tommy? Tommy? Tommy's not a butler. Tommy's just some old guy from one of your stores in Miami Beach who you dragged up here so he could keep you in secret cigars and place horse racing bets for you at Belmont Park. You're calling *that* a butler?

De Wit Dupont-Dufort He's a butler.

Marcee Dupont-Dufort (*indicating James*) *That's* a butler. A real – what's the word?

De Wit Dupont-Dufort Stuffed shirt?

Marcee Dupont-Dufort Demeanour.

De Wit Dupont-Dufort Don't talk that French to me.

Marcee Dupont-Dufort And I wish you wouldn't say 'crack-up'.

De Wit Dupont-Dufort When?

Marcee Dupont-Dufort Just now you called our – the – You called him a 'crack-up'.

De Wit Dupont-Dufort What? That butter-and-eggs out there by the pool?

Marcee Dupont-Dufort Yes. You called him a 'crack-up'.

De Wit Dupont-Dufort Well, he is.

Marcee Dupont-Dufort I know. But there's no call to actually go and say it now, is there? Especially in front of the –

De Wit Dupont-Dufort Help?

Marcee Dupont-Dufort Don't say it like that.

De Wit Dupont-Dufort Help, help, help! I'm hot!

Marcee Dupont-Dufort It's a hundred degrees.

De Wit Dupont-Dufort I could handle a drink.

Marcee Dupont-Dufort Then you should have asked 'what's-his-name'.

De Wit Dupont-Dufort It's too late.

Marcee Dupont-Dufort You're telling me.

De Wit Dupont-Dufort What's that supposed to mean?

Marcee Dupont-Dufort You'll get your drink, De Wit. As soon as the Foxes get here. I'm sure they're the kind of civilised people to offer a person a drink more than once. I mean, everybody knows it's only polite to refuse the first time you're asked.

De Wit Dupont-Dufort I'm banking on it.

Marcee Dupont-Dufort Reputation has they're as civil as civil can be.

De Wit Dupont-Dufort Reputation?

Marcee Dupont-Dufort Liz Smith.

De Wit Dupont-Dufort The gossip columnist?

Marcee Dupont-Dufort (*simultaneously*) Journalist, yes.

Marcee Dupont-Dufort I ran the list of names by her and she said of all the twenty-three prospective families this was the best. You know they live out here all year long like reclusives.

De Wit Dupont-Dufort Recluses.

Marcee Dupont-Dufort Can you imagine? Being out here in the winter? After all the parties and music and summer moves on? Not a soul around. Just you and miles and miles of empty beach and the grey ocean and hordes of locals?

De Wit Dupont-Dufort Sounds perfect.

Marcee Dupont-Dufort Perfectly awful. Just sitting out here. Kinda waiting. Don't you think? Waiting for him. Their long-lost son. Reunited to them by that paragon of social concerns, Mrs Marcee Dupont-Dufort.

De Wit Dupont-Dufort What are you talking about yourself like you're another person for?

Marcee Dupont-Dufort Just think, De Wit. There wouldn't be a home on the Upper East Side that didn't spring open to me like a tiny gold jewellery box with the right key. Pop! Dinner parties, lunch parties, brunch parties and plain old whoopee parties. The invitations would come flooding in. And one night. One winter night in the city. One winter night in the city when I'm wrapped in that fur. You know the one? The one I made you get for me last birthday? The one with my name on the lining. One winter night in that coat, and on the threshold of the Meerbaums or the Rossersteins or the Trasks or the Rockefellers, there she'd be. Linda Glass. A blur in the corner of my eye as I sail past her and hand her that same fur coat for *her* to check.

De Wit Dupont-Dufort You never cease to astound me.

Marcee Dupont-Dufort Thanks.

De Wit Dupont-Dufort That's not a compliment.

Marcee Dupont-Dufort Shove it then.

De Wit Dupont-Dufort Why didn't I have any sense of this side to you back in Miami Beach?

Marcee Dupont-Dufort Is it so bad to want to belong?

De Wit Dupont-Dufort Belonging's overrated.

Marcee Dupont-Dufort Everyone's got to belong to something, De Wit.

De Wit Dupont-Dufort Says who?

Marcee Dupont-Dufort Says me!

Mrs Fox comes into the room, followed by George Fox and his wife Valerie Fox.

Mrs Fox Says what?

Marcee Dupont-Dufort Says – nothing. Nothing at all. Absolutely nothing. We were just – Hello! I'm Marcee. Mrs – Marcee Dupont-Dufort. We spoke on the – And this. This is my husband, De Wit. De Wit Dupont-Dufort.

Mrs Fox Welcome.

Marcee Dupont-Dufort De Wit Dupont-Dufort, De Wit Dupont-Dufort –

De Wit Dupont-Dufort Hello.

Marcee Dupont-Dufort Sounds like some kinda strange language or something from Scandinavia or someplace, doesn't it?

Mrs Fox This is my son, George. George Fox.

Marcee Dupont-Dufort De Wit Dupont-Dufort, De Wit Dupont-Dufort –

George Fox Hello.

Valerie Fox Say hello, George darling.

George Fox (*simultaneously*) I did. I am.

De Wit Dupont-Dufort Likewise.

Mrs Fox And George's wife.

Valerie Fox Hi. Hello.

Mrs Fox (*simultaneously*) My daughter-in-law, Valerie.

Marcee Dupont-Dufort Hello. You have such a charming place, Mrs Fox. I mean it's so – Well, quintessential, isn't it.

Mrs Fox Is it?

Marcee Dupont-Dufort For this part of –

De Wit Dupont-Dufort I think my wife means with the shingles and the pitched roof and the views and the ocean.

Mrs Fox I'm sorry to say I forget it's there half the time.

Marcee Dupont-Dufort The house?

Mrs Fox The ocean. When the wind changes direction and I hear the breaking of the waves I sometimes think to myself: 'Oh, that's right. I live by the ocean.'

Marcee Dupont-Dufort How amazing that you might be so used to something that you forget its very existence.

Valerie Fox Especially when that thing is the ocean.

Mrs Fox My analyst –

George Fox Mother.

Mrs Fox She does, George. Dr Patchalk, says I 'do it in' by forgetting its existence.

Valerie Fox Forget the ocean. Do you even know we have a pool, George darling?

George Fox Of course I –

Valerie Fox George spends most of his time ferreting around, Mrs Dupont-Dufort –

She pronounces it 'Dupon-Dufore'.

Marcee Dupont-Dufort It's actually – You do say the 't'.

George Fox (*simultaneously*) I don't know you'd call it ferreting.

Valerie Fox Holed up in some room or other listening to his precious records.

Mrs Fox He'd have one of the largest collections of foreign recordings this side of the East River, Mrs Dupont-Dufort.

Marcee Dupont-Dufort It's actually with a 't'. At the end there.

Mrs Fox Don't you, George?

George Fox I don't know about –

Valerie Fox French! Do you speak French Mrs Dupont-Dufort?

Marcee Dupont-Dufort It's actually 'Dupont-Dufort'.

Valerie Fox (*simultaneously*) I have to say it's all 'vous, vous, vous, djer, djer, djer, escargot, merde' to me. (*And carrying straight on.*) Can we get a drink up here?

De Wit Dupont-Dufort *Now* you're talking.

George Fox (*simultaneously*) I suppose we should –

Valerie Fox (*going to the door and hollering*) James?! Do you think we could go and get some drinks up here? (*To the room.*) Buzzer's broken.

Mrs Fox Valerie, I wish you wouldn't –

Valerie Fox (*simultaneously*) Mr Dupont-Dufort?

De Wit Dupont-Dufort Bourbon. Rocks.

Valerie Fox Mrs –

Marcee Dupont-Dufort Gin with a splash of isotonic would be just grand. And it's actually – It's got a 't'.

Mrs Fox I'll have my Old Usual.

George Fox Nothing for me.

Valerie Fox George is like a camel.

George Fox (*simultaneously*) I'm just not that thirsty.

Valerie Fox Or anything really. You're just not that anything. Are you, George? (*Back to the door. Yelling.*) That's Bourbon rocks. Gin and isotonic. Old Usual for Mrs Fox and a usual usual for me. (*Back to the room. Seeing Mrs Fox's look.*) What?

Mrs Fox I do wish you wouldn't yell so, Valerie dear.

Valerie Fox (*tossing it off, taking out a cigarette*) Sorry.

Mrs Fox Please do take a seat, Mrs Dupont –

Marcee Dupont-Dufort (*about ready to pop*) There's a 't'! (*Gosh! Little too forceful. Trying to recover.*) You see. There. At the end.

Mrs Fox End of what, dear?

De Wit Dupont-Dufort (*attempt at a save*) Marcee, maybe you should cut to the –

Valerie Fox Yes. Why don't you 'cut to the' –

George Fox You can imagine that, since we received your call, Mrs Dupont-Dufort, things have been –

Valerie Fox To say the least.

George Fox (*simultaneously*) Haven't they, Mother?

Mrs Fox What?

George Fox Things have been –

Mrs Fox Of course! To be told. After all this time. After fifteen years. That –

George Fox Not that we are suggesting that this man is my –

Valerie Fox God forbid it might actually be –

George Fox (*simultaneously*) Why don't you tell us how you came upon –

Marcee Dupont-Dufort De Wit's cousin.

George Fox I beg your pardon?

De Wit Dupont-Dufort Don't blame me.

Marcee Dupont-Dufort It all started with De Wit's cousin and his experiences with Quakerism.

Mrs Fox Quakerism?

De Wit Dupont-Dufort Marcee, you don't need to go into all that.

Marcee Dupont-Dufort Context is all is what I say.

De Wit Dupont-Dufort When do you ever say that?

Marcee Dupont-Dufort Just now. So. This is the context. It concerns the war. This most recent one. Not Korea. I mean that was hardly a – I mean this last *proper* war. The one with the Nazis and the Nips –

De Wit Dupont-Dufort They know which war you mean, Marcee.

Marcee Dupont-Dufort Anyway, while most normal folks came back and reunited themselves with their wives and their kids and their jobs and their Thursday evenings at the Shalom Club or whatever –

Mrs Fox Oh!

Marcee Dupont-Dufort What?

Mrs Fox Nothing.

Marcee Dupont-Dufort Some folks came back terrifically changed. By terrifically changed I mean terrifically, terrifically changed.

De Wit Dupont-Dufort They get the drift, Marcee.

Marcee Dupont-Dufort I'm painting a picture.

De Wit Dupont-Dufort Make it a line drawing.

Marcee Dupont-Dufort Anyway, De Wit's cousin Porter was one of this last group. This terrifically changed group. He came back from Africa –

De Wit Dupont-Dufort Guam.

Marcee Dupont-Dufort Terrifically changed. And what do you know if he doesn't go and have himself some kind of nervous breakdown and ups and joins the Quakers.

Mrs Fox Goodness!

Marcee Dupont-Dufort I know! So, I don't know if you know this or not, but the Quakers are pess—

De Wit Dupont-Dufort Pacifistic.

Marcee Dupont-Dufort And, as a result of all this pess—

De Wit Dupont-Dufort Pacifistic.

Marcee Dupont-Dufort Thinking. He goes and gets himself a job working at a naval hospital in Picatinny, New Jersey, changing invalid sailors' diapers or something. I know. Don't ask. What business the Navy has having a hospital in Picatinny, New Jersey, when they're hundreds of miles from the nearest large drop of water I'll never know. But there you have it.

De Wit Dupont-Dufort It's a nut-house really.

Marcee Dupont-Dufort Sanitorium. So, Porter is being a Quaker and working in this naval –

De Wit Dupont-Dufort Nut-house.

Marcee Dupont-Dufort (*simultaneously*) Sanitorium.

Marcee Dupont-Dufort In Picatinny, New Jersey, and he gets every fourth Sunday off, and that's where we come in.

De Wit Dupont-Dufort You'll be pleased to hear.

Marcee Dupont-Dufort We're the closest thing Cousin Porter has to family in the North East, you see. So when he gets his every fourth Sunday off he comes into the city and we take him out to lunch to that place on 55th and Lex. What else is family for?

Valerie Fox Target practice?

De Wit Dupont-Dufort I don't know why we can't just go to a normal restaurant with all the other people.

Marcee Dupont-Dufort It's different, De Wit. That's why. It's modern.

Mrs Fox What do you mean, 'modern'?

Marcee Dupont-Dufort They have little plastic-fronted hutches that you take your salad or jello or whatever out of, like you're in a flying saucer or something. And the mashed potato goes right by you on a conveyor belt.

Mrs Fox Astonishing!

Valerie Fox Makes me think of rabbits.

Marcee Dupont-Dufort Doesn't it. Well, we take him there and get a booth and tell him to pick any hutch he likes and we buy him lunch.

De Wit Dupont-Dufort The place is a rip-off.

Marcee Dupont-Dufort It's neat. It's like eating lunch on the moon. Anyway, in the course of one of these monthly lunches Cousin Porter tells about this guy. This guy they've got staying out at the naval hospital in Picatinny,

New Jersey. A guy who was a soldier in the war. A guy who got himself captured by the Nazis.

Mrs Fox Good Lord!

Marcee Dupont-Dufort Apparently, they found him wandering along a French railway line in '44, and owing to a series of situations that nobody seems to know anything about, and particularly not De Wit's cousin Porter, he ends up in a prison hospital in East Germany, tucked away behind that big old iron curtain they've got there for fourteen years.

Mrs Fox This is just –

Marcee Dupont-Dufort Isn't is! Of course he'd still be there now if it wasn't for Dulles.

Mrs Fox Who?

Marcee Dupont-Dufort John Foster Dulles.

Valerie Fox The Secretary of State?

George Fox Deceased Secretary of State.

Marcee Dupont-Dufort He's dead?

De Wit Dupont-Dufort He died back in April, Marcee. Where in God's name have you been?

Marcee Dupont-Dufort Trying to get these good people their long lost son back, is where. (*To Mrs Fox.*) If I'd known he was dead I'd have sent flowers.

Valerie Fox I think it's too late for flowers.

Marcee Dupont-Dufort Well, he died having done a good thing. He died having brought back this man. Your son –

George Fox Alleged.

Marcee Dupont-Dufort Back from the misery of fourteen years in an East German prison hospital. You can only imagine.

Mrs Fox I'd rather not, Mrs Dupont-Dufort.

Marcee Dupont-Dufort It turns out that while we've been getting all hot under our collars about Korea or wherever it is, good old Secretary of State Dulles was striking up quite a friendship with all those cabbage-eating commies they have there in Moscow. They always look like funeral parlour doormen, don't they? Anyway, Secretary Dulles and these funeral parlour doormen come to some kinda arrangement whereby we release some of their red spies we have stuffed away in our military prisons in exchange for them releasing some of our boys they've got stuffed away in theirs.

Valerie Fox I'm beginning to see –

De Wit Dupont-Dufort Marcee's like San Francisco in summer, Mrs Fox. Sooner or later the fog has to lift.

Marcee Dupont-Dufort Exactly. So, a few months later an airplane arrives at a naval base in western New Jersey carrying a bunch of our boys home. Including your –

George Fox Mrs Dupont –

Marcee Dupont-Dufort *This* man.

Mrs Fox And this was relayed to you over lunch in a cafeteria?

Marcee Dupont-Dufort Oh no, it's a proper restaurant. They just have food in hutches.

George Fox There's one thing that doesn't make sense, Mrs Dupont-Dufort.

De Wit Dupont-Dufort *One* thing?

George Fox Why has this man not been repatriated?

Marcee Dupont-Dufort Which?

De Wit Dupont-Dufort Reunited –

George Fox Yes. With his family.

Marcee Dupont-Dufort Why? Oh, God! With all this – That's the thing, you see. The big thing. The thing they must have discovered very early on. The thing is – Well, I am so sorry, Mr Fox. I neglected to – I just assumed –

Valerie Fox What? What is it?

Marcee Dupont-Dufort This man. The thing is. This man has no memory! (*Stunned.*) None. Nothing. Nothing up to the point he was found on those French railway tracks and carried off into deepest darkest Germany. They called him Gene.

Valerie Fox Gene?

Marcee Dupont-Dufort Short for Eugene.

Mrs Fox Eugene?

Marcee Dupont-Dufort Apparently one of the reds at the prison hospital in East Germany was a theatre buff and liked plays by Eugene O'Neill. Frankly there's no accounting for taste. We saw one once, didn't we, De Wit?

De Wit Dupont-Dufort Did we?

Marcee Dupont-Dufort There was so much wailing and carrying on, and awful socialistic raving and children wanting to do the most unnatural things to their parents and parents doing the most ungodly things to their children, that we didn't stay for the second half.

De Wit Dupont-Dufort I don't remem—

Marcee Dupont-Dufort You slept through the first.

Mrs Fox Just as well by the sounds, Mr Dupont-Dufort.

Valerie Fox And this . . . man?

Marcee Dupont-Dufort Gene. Yes?

Valerie Fox He remembers . . .

Marcee Dupont-Dufort Nothing. It's as if a great wall were put up in his brain and everything prior to that French railroad track is on the other side of it and can't be gotten at.

George Fox Men see things during wartime.

Marcee Dupont-Dufort What was that?

George Fox Men. Have experiences. That might make it –

Marcee Dupont-Dufort Yes, yes. I suppose so. Anyway, it's while Cousin Porter is telling us this over his salad and mashed potato that it hits me. Orphaned dogs!

Mrs Fox Excuse me?

De Wit Dupont-Dufort You better buckle up for this one.

Marcee Dupont-Dufort No. Listen. It did. You know it did, De Wit. You see when De Wit and I met. This was in Miami Beach and De Wit decided it was time –

De Wit Dupont-Dufort It was more or less decided for me.

Marcee Dupont-Dufort Nobody likes a man without ambition, De Wit.

Valerie Fox Except the communists, I suppose.

Marcee Dupont-Dufort Exactly. So, being a good patriot, De Wit decides to expand his little stores into the great North East.

Mrs Fox Delicatessens, yes?

De Wit Dupont-Dufort Department stores.

Marcee Dupont-Dufort To begin with there was a lot to be done. Stores to be opened and a home to be made. But after a while. I mean, De Wit had the store and golf and Rotary. But me? What did I have? There's only so much mah-jong a person can play. So, I decided to dedicate my life to orphaned dogs.

Valerie Fox You don't say.

Marcee Dupont-Dufort You wouldn't credit how many orphaned dogs there are in the city. Especially after the major holidays. Dropped at the pound or just dumped in boxes behind Chinese restaurants. It's a disgrace.

Mrs Fox I see.

Marcee Dupont-Dufort So, a few of us got together and started a little charity for the protection and rehousing of orphaned dogs. 'PAWS FOR THOUGHT'.

Valerie Fox P – A . . .

De Wit Dupont-Dufort W – S.

Marcee Dupont-Dufort Exactly! So, when Cousin Porter mentioned this man. This Gene person. I thought, how is that so different to –

Mrs Fox Dogs.

Marcee Dupont-Dufort And I decided I'd make it my business to find a real forever home for him. Just like a dog.

De Wit Dupont-Dufort Woof, woof!

James comes in with a tray of drinks.

Valerie Fox At last.

Mrs Fox Thank you, James.

De Wit Dupont-Dufort Just what the doctor sent for.

Valerie Fox James, is Mr . . . The gentleman alright out there?

Marcee Dupont-Dufort De Wit thought he should just come straight on in, but I thought it might be a little easier for him if we chatted first.

Mrs Fox Of course.

De Wit Dupont-Dufort Is he still moping around beside the pool?

James Not exactly, sir.

Mrs Fox What are you saying, James?

James He's more half in, ma'am.

Valerie Fox For goodness sake, James, don't be obscure.

James He's taken off his shoes and socks and rolled up his trousers and is sitting on the edge with his legs dangling in the water.

Marcee Dupont-Dufort I'm so sorry, Mrs Fox. I had no idea he'd start out taking liberties.

Mrs Fox Don't mention it. The man is hot. Why shouldn't he take off his shoes and socks and dangle his feet in the pool. James?

James Yes, ma'am?

Mrs Fox Tell him to come on up.

James Yes, ma'am.

He goes.

George Fox I hope you don't mind me saying, Mrs Dupont-Dufort, but I don't understand how it is you managed to convince the United States Navy to hand over this, this, this –

Valerie Fox Man, George. You *can* say it. Man. Man.

George Fox With all due respect a charity for orphaned dogs hardly qualifies you as a social worker or private investigator. Surely there were already methods in place to have his real family located and to have him delivered safely back to them.

Marcee Dupont-Dufort Oh, the Navy tried. In the way huge bureaucratic governmental monstrosities try. An ad in the newspapers! I mean, they didn't even include a photograph for heaven's sake! Honestly. Governments! We should just do away with the whole lot of them!

Mrs Fox Hear, hear!

Marcee Dupont-Dufort No. Getting our hands on him turned out to be a piece of cake.

Valerie Fox How then?

Marcee Dupont-Dufort 'Serviceman for a Day'.

Mrs Fox 'Serviceman' . . .

De Wit Dupont-Dufort Crack-up for a weekend more like.

Marcee Dupont-Dufort We do the same with dogs.

Mrs Fox This is at . . .

Marcee Dupont-Dufort 'PAWS FOR THOUGHT', yes. Before we find the dogs a forever home we let them go home with families. Overnight. You see? Gives people a chance to get to know the dogs. So, turns out the VA has the same kinda thing going on. Except instead of dogs it's servicemen. Servicemen who are incapacitated and away from their families. Or like in this fella's case has no family at all, or no memory of one at least. You get assigned one. A serviceman and you go visit and take them brownies or bring them out to the park or Coney Island or –

De Wit Dupont-Dufort Just like dogs but less chance they'll go doo-doo on the rug.

Marcee Dupont-Dufort So, we get Cousin Porter to recommend us to the programme as fine upstanding kinds of folks, which of course we are, and before we know it we're face to face with our very own 'Serviceman for a Day'.

De Wit Dupont-Dufort He's a real barrel of laughs, let me tell you.

Valerie Fox But why us? What makes you think this, this, this –

Marcee Dupont-Dufort Gene.

George Fox Person.

Valerie Fox May be –

Marcee Dupont-Dufort Process of illumin—

De Wit Dupont-Dufort Elimination.

Marcee Dupont-Dufort That's right. Our first meeting I noticed it right away.

Valerie Fox What?

Marcee Dupont-Dufort The accent. Good 'Old Long Island' family accent.

Mrs Fox We have an accent?

Marcee Dupont-Dufort Confirmed by a speech podiat—

De Wit Dupont-Dufort Pathologist.

Marcee Dupont-Dufort We took him to on one of his visits. Then, it was just a matter of matching the records of the missing with the approximate dates of the disappearance in France, along with descriptions of the men. Five foot whatever. Brown hair. Blue eyes. Blah, blah, blah. And before we knew it. A list!

Mrs Fox A list?

Marcee Dupont-Dufort Twenty-three families from Montauk to Manhasset with a couple of Iowans with Long Island lineage thrown in for good measure. Oh. And a Californian with a Long Island connection. But I'm sure they're not it.

Mrs Fox And you're beginning with us?

Marcee Dupont-Dufort Mrs Fox, I'm going to be frank with you.

Mrs Fox I wish you would.

Marcee Dupont-Dufort You seem like decent people. The right *kind* of people. There's something about this man. This Gene. He smacks of the right *kind* of people. And, frankly, he smacks of you.

Mrs Fox I don't know what to – If only Dr Patchalk were –

George Fox You pay us a great compliment, Mrs Dupont-Dufort. I'm sure you can appreciate it's been a long time. Fifteen years since we were first notified he was missing.

Valerie Fox Then. Nothing. No body. Nothing to bring home. Not a single. Solitary –

George Fox Yes?

Valerie Fox You know what I mean.

Mrs Fox Why even the Wilders got given a heel bone, didn't they?

George Fox Then. To receive your call.

Marcee Dupont-Dufort Of course.

George Fox It was a shock.

Marcee Dupont-Dufort Of course.

Suddenly Juliette comes in, breathless.

Mrs Fox What is it, Juliette?

Juliette I'm sorry. I just thought –

Mrs Fox What?

Juliette The glasses.

45

Mrs Fox Alright. Go ahead.

Valerie Fox Juliette, have you seen James with the –
gentleman?

Juliette No. I thought he'd be in here with you all.

Valerie Fox Well, he's not. Obviously.

George Fox The fact is, Mrs Dupont-Dufort, the chances
that this poor fellow is my – Our – Are pretty remote.

Mrs Fox Yes. As much as I long to hold my dearest son
to me once more, to nestle his head hard against my
breast, to protect him from the psychic winds of fate, I
fear what's likely to transpire is a pleasant but ultimately
disappointing exchange with an ex-serviceman.

Marcee Dupont-Dufort With all due respects, Mrs Fox,
I'm sure it won't.

Mrs Fox And I'm sure I read someplace that a mother
was meant to have certain innate feelings about such
things. Is she not?

Valerie Fox For God's . . . The suspense is just –

Mrs Fox *Please* stay calm, Valerie.

Valerie Fox Well, where is he already?

Mrs Fox Adults wait, Valerie, dear. Only children
demand to be seen to at once –

The following five speeches all simultaneous:

Valerie Fox Then I guess I'm not much of an adult then.
Cos if James doesn't bring that man up here this instant
I tell you my head is going to fly right off the top of my
shoulders. Pop!

Mrs Fox (*simultaneously*) The bearing of the yolk of
frustration is the great mark of adulthood. So said Freud.
You simply need to manage your own frustrations,

46

Valerie. Try a few deep breaths –

George Fox (*simultaneously*) I don't see why you're so worked up over a man who is going to mean no more to you than a stranger you might pass in the street. Can you tell me that?

Marcee Dupont-Dufort (*simultaneously*) I don't mean to be the cause of any friction here, Mrs Fox. De Wit, don't smoke those in here.

De Wit Dupont-Dufort (*simultaneously*) I'm gonna take this opportunity to have a cigar. Anybody mind if I have a cigar? Yes? No?

And in the midst of the cacophony James enters the room. On Valerie's 'Pop!' they all turn to look at him.

Valerie Fox Well?

James He was just . . .

Slowly, Gene peers around the corner. He takes a few steps gingerly into the room. His trousers are rolled up. He carries his shoes and socks in his hands.

Mrs Fox Is that . . . Jack?

Gene smiles weakly. He looks like he might be about to answer. Then, just as he takes a breath to speak, his eyes roll back in his head and he keels over in a dead faint.

Black.
    And Serge Gainsbourg sings . . . 'Cha Cha Cha du Loup'.

Two

A bedroom on the second floor of that same Long Island estate house. Once, it belonged to a young man. Single bed. Armchair. A large armoire with a mirrored door. Perhaps a window or a glass door leads out on to a little balcony with a view down to the terrace and the pool, and beyond to the dunes and the ocean, winking as ever in the late afternoon heat. The sky is low. A storm far out to sea. In that same echoing distance as before, Serge Gainsbourg sings 'Cha Cha Cha du Loup'.

Gene is sitting bolt upright in bed. It is as if a small boy had suddenly exploded into sweaty manhood.

Mrs Fox . . . And then there's the Dupont-Duforts. Really, there's no point in them heading back along the Long Island Expressway this late in the day. They'll be in rush-hour traffic the minute they hit Idlewild and won't set eyes on the city before midnight. So, they might as well stay in the pool house. I've asked Juliette to see what she can do about supper. Bearing in mind the kitchen contains pretty much tinned dogs and frozen TV dinners. It's best to have low expectations is what I suppose I'm saying, dear. And being as how it's your first night back here with us at, well – home, I thought you might want to dress. Some of your old – I don't know. You look a little – All that communist prison food I don't doubt. I'm sure there'll be something in the armoire. James here is going to help. Aren't you –

Gene Shh!

Mrs Fox What's that, dear?

Gene Shhh!

48

Mrs Fox Why, Jack, you seem to have sprung a leak.

Gene There!

Mrs Fox What?

Gene There!

Mrs Fox Where?

Gene Some kind of – There!

Mrs Fox The music, you mean?

Gene French.

Mrs Fox Oh, that's just George.

Gene George?

Mrs Fox Your brother.

Gene I got a brother?

Mrs Fox *Have* a brother. And of course you do. He carried you up here.

Gene He did?

Mrs Fox Along with James and the other gentleman.

James Took us some time to get you up those stairs, sir, seeing as how you was such a dead weight.

Mrs Fox They thought it might help for you to be put up here amongst your old things and whatnots. I must say they gave your head a good old whack against the what's-it there as they carried you in, but Mrs Dupont-Dufort said it was impossible to think that any whack could do greater damage than that which had already been done.

Gene I was carried in here?

Mrs Fox When you passed out. Yes.

Gene I passed out?

Mrs Fox Flat out as a pancake. George –

Gene My brother.

Mrs Fox That's right. And Mr Dupont-Dufort. And James here. You do remember James, don't you?

Gene Do I? Yes, from by the pool before.

Mrs Fox Well, yes. From practically forever. James has been with us since you were a little blob in diapers.

James You gave us an awful shock, Master Fox.

Mrs Fox Oh, I'm sure it'd be Sergeant Fox by now, James, don't you think?

James If you say so, ma'am. Sergeant Fox.

Mrs Fox You might as well get something outta all those years in the services sitting in that nasty old East German prison hospital eating sauerkraut, don't you think? I'm sure they'd have made you a sergeant by now.

Gene I'm not so sure –

Mrs Fox Major then?

Gene I'm not entirely –

Mrs Fox Perhaps you're right. Let's split the difference and call it Captain.

Gene Captain?

Mrs Fox Captain Fox! It has a certain something. Don't you –

Gene Who are you?

Stunned something.

Mrs Fox What?

Gene Who are you?

Mrs Fox Well, I'm your mother of course.

Gene *You're* my mother?

Mrs Fox Jack, you're being silly. You must recognise your own mother for goodness sake. Tell him, James.

James She sure is your mother, Master –

Mrs Fox James!

James *Captain* Fox.

Mrs Fox You see, Jack?

Gene And my name is –

Mrs Fox Jack, of course. What did you *think* your name was? Gene?

She wrings the name out derisively like a wet towel.

Gene (*trying it on*) Jack.

Mrs Fox That's right, dear. Jack Fox. It's the name I gave you. The name your father and I gave you.

Gene I have a father?

Mrs Fox Had. He passed just after peace was declared in the first war.

Gene I'm sorry for your loss.

Mrs Fox And I for yours. He was run over by his own out-of-control armoured motorcycle moments after the Armistice was signed.

Gene Good God!

Mrs Fox Too strong a death drive, according to Dr Patchalk. At least it was mercifully quick. Thanks to the armour. James?

James Yes, ma'am?

Mrs Fox I'm going to go down and see how Juliette is getting on with defrosting supper. You stay here and help Captain Fox sort through the armoire. See if you can find something for him to wear that doesn't look like we've thrown a bedsheet over a malnourished child.

James Yes, ma'am.

Mrs Fox (*to Gene*) Then when you're good and ready, you come downstairs and have a nice highball or something and a thawed-out frozen TV dinner and we'll get on with the business of being a family, alright?

    She heads for the door.

But really, you know, I think I'm handling the whole situation so well, don't you?

    And Mrs Fox has gone, closing the door behind her.

Gene *What* was that?

James (*beginning to lay out clothes from the armoire*) I believe *that* was your mother, Captain Fox, sir.

Gene I see. Well . . . (*Sizing up the room.*) I suppose I should – I should – I should –

James Yes, sir?

Gene The truth is James, I don't know what 'I suppose I should'.

James Perhaps you could bathe, sir?

Gene Bathe?

James Before dressing for dinner?

Gene Well . . . I suppose I *could* bathe.

James You gotta tub.

Gene I do?

James Through there.

Gene (*going into the bathroom*) Through . . .

James Yes, sir.

Gene (*off*) Holy crap!

James You alright, sir?

Gene (*coming back in.*) That tub's the size of an Olympic swimming pool.

James That so, sir.

Gene Suppose it wouldn't hurt to do a few laps.

James Don't suppose it would, sir. (*Heading to the bathroom.*) I'll go run it for you.

James goes into the bathroom. The sound of running water. Gene pads around the room. He picks up a photograph in a frame of a fat baby. Pulls a face. Sets it down. He picks up the suit that has been laid out on the bed.

Gene You know, James, perhaps this Jack Fox situation is not such a bad situation, situation-wise.

James (*off*) How's that, sir?

Gene I mean, tub the size of an Olympic swimming pool. Frozen TV dinners. Guy to run your bathwater and tell you what to wear. Could be worse. Could be a whole lot worse.

James (*off*) Surely could be, sir.

Gene holds the suit up and looks at himself in the mirror.

Gene Well, hello there. Captain Jack Fox, huh? Handsome son-of-a –

The hall door flies open and George stalks in. He's particularly clenched.

Hi.

James (*off*) What's that, sir?

George Fox (*glowering at Gene*) Huh!

He turns on his heels and stalks back out of the room. Gene is left a little dazed. James comes in.

James Bath running, sir.

Gene What?

James Your bath.

Gene Oh, thanks, thanks.

James Laid out a robe in there for you as well.

Gene Thanks a million. (*A little concerned.*) Tell me, James. What's he like, anyway? This, this, this . . . Jack Fox? Personality-wise. Decent fella, is he?

James (*busying himself at the armoire.*) Well, I suppose he's not unlike yourself, sir.

Gene Well, that's a start, isn't it? To be told that the person you may very well turn out to be is not unlike the person you basically already are?

James Yes, sir.

Gene If only I could just – (*Trying to wring something from his memory. Perhaps back at the photograph.*) It's no use. I might as well be on Mars.

James Mars. Hamptons. Some folks say there's little difference.

Gene Gotta be *something* around here that rings a bell, memory-wise.

He heads into the bathroom. Coming out immediately.

You know what it's like, James?

James No, sir.

Gene It's like jigsaw puzzles. You like jigsaw puzzles?

James No, sir, can't say I do.

Gene That's a shame, cos this is like that.

James How so, sir?

Gene Putting together Jack Fox's life. My life here with you. Like a giant jigsaw puzzle.

He goes into the bathroom. He comes out immediately.

Only one thing.

James What's that, sir?

Gene We don't have any of the pieces.

James Not sure how you're going to put together a jigsaw puzzle without the pieces, sir.

Gene Simple. Gonna have to be a regular Perry Mason, James.

James That so.

Gene Gonna to have to interrogate everyone from his – *my* past. To see if we can find some of those missing jigsaw puzzle pieces.

He goes into the bathroom.

James If you say so, Captain Fox, sir.

Gene immediately comes out of the bathroom.

Gene James?

James Yes, sir?

Gene Do you think you might stop calling me 'sir' and 'Captain Fox' and the like. It's giving me the heebies.

James What would you like me to call you, sir?

Gene I don't know. I suppose – How's 'bout Gene?

James Not sure Mrs Fox would appreciate me doing that, sir.

Gene For the time being. Something tells me – Just. For the time being. OK?

James I'll do my best, Captain Fox.

Gene Thanks.

And Gene is gone into the bathroom. He closes the door behind him. James is still at the armoire.
The door to the hallway flies open and Valerie is standing there, drink in hand. She scans the room.

James Yes, ma'am?

Valerie Fox Just checking, James.

James For?

Valerie Fox Rats.

She leaves as fast as she came in. James goes back to the armoire. To choose a tie perhaps.
The hall door flies open and Juliette is standing there. James doesn't need to turn around to know who it is.

James Pool house?

Juliette Done.

James Dinner?

Juliette On. Is he . . .

James Taking a bath.

Juliette (*coming into the room properly*) A miracle.

James No miracle.

Juliette Resurrected from the dead.

James Never *dead* to start with.

Juliette Like a zombie.

James You been watching too much TV.

Juliette He recognised me, you know.

James When?

Juliette When you and the rest were carrying him up here and I was holding the door. Just before you went and whacked his head. He opened his eyes for a second and –

James What?

Juliette He recognised me.

James He didn't *recognise* you.

Juliette He did too.

James That man in there didn't recognise you any more than he'd recognise a kind word!

The water is turned off. They freeze. Then . . .

Here. (*The clothes.*) Make yourself useful.

She does.

Juliette Was always kind to me.

James Humph!

Juliette What's that supposed to mean?

James Keep your voice down.

Juliette What's that supposed to mean?

James It means that in '44 when we heard that that man taking a bath in there was gone from us? There was a moment when –

Juliette What?

James I was glad of it, is what! And so were a good many other folks besides!

Suddenly the door to the bathroom flies open and Gene springs into the room in the bathrobe. He hasn't yet bathed.

Gene James, I was just thinking that I should probably – (*Seeing Juliette.*) Oh! Pardon me.

James You remember Juliette, sir?

Gene Hi.

Juliette Hi. I mean, hello, Mr –

James It's Captain.

Juliette Captain Fox.

Gene Gene.

Juliette No, Juliette.

Gene What? No, *me*. Gene.

Juliette Gene?

Gene Please. Call me Gene.

Juliette (*turning to James*) But, why would I . . .

Gene For the time being.

Juliette Gene?

Gene Until we can be sure.

Juliette (*to James*) Is this some kind of –

James This is no kind of nothing. Mister – Captain Fox here wishes to be addressed as Gene.

Juliette Gene.

Gene Gene. That's right.

Juliette (*carefully, as if she were speaking a foreign language*) Hello. Gene.

Gene Hello.

James Juliette here was just giving me a hand with some of your –

Gene I'm known to you, am I?

James (*out the side of his mouth*) 'Recognised' you, did he?

Juliette (*out the side of hers*) Shut – (*Quickly to Gene, and still talking like English may be her second language.*) Yes. Yes, you are known to me.

Gene Well, this is just perfect. I'll begin with you.

Juliette Begin with . . .

Gene Juliette, you might as well know that before I assume the mantle of this Jack Fox, I intend on interrogating each and every person who claims to have known me. Him. In order to ascertain if there is anything that might ring a bell and *ergo* if I am indeed he. Me. You get my drift?

James You better go on and start interrogating somebody else, Captain, sir. Juliette here's gotta get the pool house all set for Mr and Mrs Dupont –

Juliette Done.

James Then there's the supper that Mrs Fox –

Juliette On.

James Looks as if there's a storm coming and there's all that pool furniture to be brought –

Juliette It's brought.

Gene Seems like she's free to chat then.

Juliette (*beaming at James*) Free as a little birdie.

Gene Good. Let's get down to it right away. Please. Take a seat.

Juliette I'd only be too pleased to do so.

James Mrs Fox doesn't like the staff to sit when they're in the presence of the –

Gene James, perhaps you might excuse us. Just for a short while. That way I may have the opportunity to interrogate her unmolested.

Juliette (*sniggering*) Molested.

James (*quickly to Juliette*) '*Un*' means not!

Gene Thank you, James.

James If you need me –

Gene I'll ring.

Juliette You'll have to yell. Buzzer's broken. Don't be shy. They all do it.

Gene Loud and clear.

James I laid out your –

Gene And as soon as I'm finished with Juliette here I shall have my bath and don my suit for supper –

Juliette It's just dogs.

Gene And make my way to wherever these 'dogs' are being offered.

James You'll find that that's in the dining room, sir, which is –

Gene I'm sure it will all come flooding back to me presently. Thank you, James.

And James is gone, leaving the hall door open behind him. Gene turns back to the room and is confronted with a beaming Juliette.

Gene Well . . .

Juliette Hi.

Gene So, Juliette, you understand what it is I'm attempting to do here?

Juliette Oh, I understand alright.

Gene Good. So –

Juliette (*she's going to burst, delighting in teasing him on his choice of name*) Gene! For Pete's sake!

Suddenly George comes in with a long wooden box.

George Fox My mother wanted you to – (*Upon seeing Juliette.*) Oh!

Juliette (*springing up*) Mr George. We were just – I know I was sitting, but Gene here –

George Fox Gene?

Juliette Wanted to ask me some questions unmolested.

Gene What? No! I was taking a bath.

George Fox Of course.

Gene And I thought I should carry out a –

Juliette (*proud as can be*) He's going to do a full exploratory examination.

George Fox I could save him the trouble.

Gene You could?

George Fox Any doubt I may have had about his personage has just this minute been dispelled.

Gene It has?

George Fox Go on and tell him, Juliette.

Juliette Tell him what?

George Fox That he is Jack Fox.

Juliette Well, he does bear his looks.

George Fox You see?

Juliette And he does have his air somewhat.

George Fox You see?

Juliette (*flatly*) But it ain't him!

George Fox What?

Juliette This man says his name is Gene.

George Fox You been hittin' the hop?

Juliette He *says* his name is *Gene*.

Gene Just until we can be sure.

George Fox You really expect us to believe –

Gene Look, Mr Fox – George. I can assure you, I'm not insensitive to how this must be for you and your –

George Fox Oh, good.

Gene To have lost a brother. Believed him dead. Then to have him pop up. Like this. Outta, outta, outta New Jersey. I mean, I mean, I mean . . . (*Searching to prove his sensitivity.*) Think about how it must have been for you and your family. Firstly to be told that he was missing. Vanished altogether.

Juliette Heartbreaking.

Gene Then to be told that you should assume he's dead. Lying in some continental mass grave someplace.

Juliette Awful.

Gene I mean, I mean, I mean – Think about the pain.

Juliette The pain, Mr George.

Gene And before that. The sad farewell.

Juliette 'Farewell, farewell.'

Gene His final night under this very roof. In this very room, perhaps.

Juliette Tucked up in this teeny bed maybe.

Gene The family gathered around. The tearful mother, desperate to spend that last night with him before he marches off first thing –

George Fox She was at a card evening.

Gene (*simultaneously*) – heading for places unknown and fates undreamt – What?

George Fox She was at a card evening.

Gene A what?

George Fox You know. Women get together. Play cards.

Gene I am aware of the nature of a card evening.

George Fox It might have been charades. No. No, it was a Thursday. That's definitely cards.

Gene But her son was –

George Fox You weren't speaking.

Gene I . . .

George Fox By then.

Gene By . . .

George Fox Hadn't for months and months.

Gene (*indicating Juliette*) Perhaps not in front of –

George Fox Oh, God! It was common knowledge, wasn't it, Juliette?

Juliette Uh-huh. (*To Gene.*) Most everybody knew. You sure can paint an affecting picture though.

Gene But. A card evening? How is that possible? I – *He* was leaving this house to go to war. Perhaps forever.

George Fox Nevertheless, a great silence had descended between you both. (*Thrusting the box at him.*) Here. She. Our mother – My – Whatever you wanna call her. She thought *this* might help.

Gene (*holding the box, still in a daze*) This?

George Fox I'll leave you two to get back to your exploratory investigations.

Gene Yes. What? No, you don't –

And George is gone, closing the door behind him.

Juliette How'd I do?

Gene (*about to open the box*) What?

Juliette How'd I do?

Gene I don't –

Juliette It's pretty clever. I'll say that much.

Gene It is?

Juliette How long you planning on keeping it up?

Gene What 'up'?

Juliette Anyway, they're not gonna hear a peep outta me.

Gene About what?

Juliette About Atlantic City.

Gene Atlantic City?

Juliette Or Vegas.

Gene Vegas?

Juliette Or that friend of your momma's.

Gene Which friend?

Juliette That awful Upper East-Sider with the face like pulled taffy. The one you managed to get all of that dough outta to pay off those fellas.

Gene I did? He did? Which fellas?

Juliette The fellas from Atlantic City, of course.

Gene Of course.

Juliette And Vegas.

Gene Of course.

Juliette Mind you. She sure did come after your momma for that money after you were shipped off.

Gene Who?

Juliette Ole Taffy-Face.

Gene Good 'Ole Taffy-Face'.

Juliette Why these rooms are as empty as they are.

Gene They are?

Juliette is in full swing now. Enjoying that she has all this knowledge.

Juliette They've been selling stuff off for years to pay off your debts. Broker comes in from the city every coupla of months or so and takes bits and pieces back with him. I have the devil's own time rearranging the furniture to make the rooms look even halfway full. Lugging all this stuff around getting me man's arms. (*And proffering a biceps.*) Take a feel.

Gene I'd rather not.

Juliette What do I care. I was practically outta here anyway. Before you showed up.

Gene Before I –

Juliette What'd you think? I was going to spend my life just sitting out here at the end of nowhere? There are other things I can do, you know.

Gene I'm sure.

Juliette In the city. I know people, you know. I've been taking notes. Pages and pages. Who knows? I just may go and write something. A book. A play even. I'm not stupid.

Gene Glad to hear it.

Juliette That's how I know what it is you're doing.

Gene What am I doing?

Juliette Quit it! It's me, dummy! You're pretending to be this amnesiac. This Gene person. So the lawyers or debt collectors or whoever won't come after you. You must have sprung a leak when that awful Dupont-Dufort ferreted you out. Although why you'd want to hide out in New Jersey I'll never know. Anyway, it's OK. Your secret's safe with me.

Gene It is?

Juliette Same as ours.

Gene Ours. What?!

Juliette Secret, stupid.

Gene We have a secret?

Juliette If it wasn't so cute, I'd go straight and slap your face.

Gene And is our secret anywhere near as terrifying as I think it might be?

Juliette I'm too old now, is that it?

Gene No. Well, yes. But no.

Juliette I loved every minute, you know.

Gene You did?

Juliette Even when I was screaming.

Gene You were?

Juliette I knew it made me special.

Gene It did? You are. You were. I'm sure. Screaming?

Juliette It *is* that I'm too old.

Gene No.

Juliette It's that I'm twenty-nine.

Gene No.

Juliette Alright, thirty.

Gene No.

Juliette I know it's not exactly fifteen.

Gene No. What? He was conducting some kinda courtship with a fifteen-year-old?

Juliette Oh, God no.

Gene Thank God!

Juliette (*offended at his assumption of appropriateness*) It wasn't a courtship! I was a maid, for Pete's sake! We were just screwing around in the laundry closet, that's all!

Gene Good God!

Juliette Anyway, I got a bag all packed and ready to go. You just say the word. OK?

The hall door flies open and Mrs Fox sails in, dressed for dinner and carrying a necklace.

Mrs Fox I wanted to come in and check to see that George – (*Seeing Juliette.*) Oh –

Juliette I was just helping Gene here with his things.

Gene I'd – Yes. She. Very kindly –

Mrs Fox Juliette you're to refer to Captain Fox as Captain Fox, do you understand?

Juliette But, Captain Fox has asked to be addressed as Gene.

Mrs Fox I don't care whether Captain Fox has asked to be addressed as Julius Rosenberg, he has a perfectly good name and we should use it.

Gene Given the circumstances at this stage I think perhaps Gene would be preferable.

Juliette See?

Mrs Fox Balderdash.

Gene I'm sorry, but if you refer to me as Captain Fox I shall simply not respond.

Mrs Fox Juliette, as long as I am the one signing your cheque at the end of every month you will refer to Captain Fox by whatever name *I* so choose, alright?

Juliette Alright. Captain Fox?

Gene Yes? I mean, no. I mean, I'm not hearing a word you're saying.

Juliette Welcome home, Captain Fox.

Gene (*involuntarily*) Thank you. (*Then.*) Damn it!

Juliette beams and is gone.

Mrs Fox Good to have that all worked out, Jack dear. (*Indicating the necklace.*) Here. Do this up for me, would you?

Gene Um – alright.

He takes the necklace and stands behind Mrs Fox attempting to do it up.

Mrs Fox It was a gift from your late father.

Gene (*struggling with the necklace*) Do you think we might have the opportunity –

Mrs Fox Many's the time as a young boy you would stand behind me as you do now, doing me up as you now do. I thought I would wear it in honour of you and he tonight.

Gene Yes. Well. On that, I wonder if I might speak to you about –

George comes in, dressed for dinner.

George Fox I've been sent up to say –

Mrs Fox George darling! Look at what a good boy your brother Jack is being? Fixing me up like this. Just like old times. Don't you think?

George Fox Dogs are up.

He turns to go.

Gene Actually, Mr Fox – George. If you wouldn't mind staying there's one or two –

Mrs Fox Yes. Do stay, George darling. Perhaps you can do a better job of getting a two-cent hook through a cheap silver eye than your brother here.

Gene (*completely frustrated by the necklace*) It's –

Mrs Fox (*to George, low and authoritative*) Take over.

He does as Valerie comes in, cocktail in hand.

Gene There's actually something I want to –

Valerie Fox Well, hail, hail!

Mrs Fox Yes. 'The gang's all here'. Cocktail hour already, Valerie?

Valerie Fox I thought I'd come and check up on –

George Fox (*fussing with the necklace*) I bet you did.

Valerie Fox If I'd known you were all ferreted away up here I'd have had James wheel the drinks trolley right on up. I'll give him a yell.

Mrs Fox Please, don't –

Valerie Fox (*yelling out of the hall door*) James? James? Do bring a tray of drinks up to Master Jack's room would you? It seems we're having cocktails in the eaves this evening! (*Back in the room.*) Like it's not hot enough downstairs.

George Fox Hot air rises.

Mrs Fox Val knows that, don't you, dear? And it's Captain Fox, now.

Valerie Fox Been given a promotion, has he?

Mrs Fox (*the necklace*) Fussing, George, for heaven's sake!

George Fox It's coming, it's coming.

Valerie Fox Where have I heard that before.

Mrs Fox Val dear, if you mean to be here at all, take over from your husband and do me up, will you?

Valerie Fox You heard your mommy.

She takes over.

Mrs Fox Clearly the fastening of women's jewellery should only ever be trusted to other women and little boys.

Valerie Fox (*done*) There!

Mrs Fox At last!

Gene (*who has been quietly steeling himself to intervene and is sounding a little desperate*) Please!

Mrs Fox Please what, dear?

Gene Do you think I might have the opportunity of saying something?

Mrs Fox Well, of course, dear. Jack has something to say, you two. Gather round, gather round. George, a chair.

George Fox Yes, Mother.

She takes a seat.

Mrs Fox Go ahead, dear.

Suddenly Gene is the centre of attention.

Gene I don't wish to appear rude.

Mrs Fox Then don't, dear.

Gene Yes. Well. Firstly, I'd like to thank you.

Mrs Fox You're welcome. What for precisely?

Gene Your hospitality for one. It's very kind of you to put me up here.

Mrs Fox Well, where else would we put you dear? That two-bit motel on the Montauk Highway run by lesbians? This *is* your home, after all.

Gene Well, yes. We'll get to that.

Mrs Fox To *what* exactly?

Gene When I came to just now in this bed –

Mrs Fox *Your* bed, yes.

Gene And was told that I may well be this, this, this –

Valerie Fox Jack Fox.

Gene Thank you. I was frankly overcome. Emotions-wise.

Mrs Fox Naturally.

Gene It seemed incredible to think that all this –

Mrs Fox All what?

Gene This room and house and pool and park and beach and James – This whole Long Island life could be mine.

Mrs Fox Well, I can only imagine after New Jersey –

Gene (*jumping on this*) Yes! Especially after New Jersey! The hospital. A kind of – well, prison really. All their horrific methodologies for trying to unearth who it is you might actually be. You end up feeling like a kinda – kinda – goldfish or something.

Mrs Fox Tragic. You boys had goldfish, didn't you? As children?

George Fox Mother.

Gene So, you can imagine that after all that, I was, let's say, momentarily titillated by the idea that I could be this, this, this –

Valerie Fox Jack Fox.

Gene Thank you.

Mrs Fox (*getting up to go*) Isn't it wonderful! Let's get you dressed and downstairs and we can all have a nice long catch-up.

Gene The thing is, I have just now heard one or two facts from – From certain members of the domestic staff –

Valerie Fox Which staff?

Mrs Fox We can hardly trust the discernment of your true character to tales by the help, Jack.

Gene The thing is, these 'facts' leave me in some serious doubt as to whether I am in fact this, this, this –

Valerie Fox Jack Fox.

Gene As they are – Thank you – Facts that don't at all chime with the kind of person I feel myself to be, personality-wise. Frankly, and without wishing to create offence, what's a fella to do? Trust his true identity to the assertions of a bunch of strangers?

Mrs Fox *This* is *precisely* why I sent George up here with your little present, Jack.

Gene My present?

Mrs Fox If you can't be persuaded by your own flesh and blood, or *strangers* as you'd prefer to call us, perhaps something more concrete will awaken you.

Gene What are you –

Mrs Fox George brought it to you, didn't he?

George Fox It's over –

Mrs Fox (*pouncing on the long wooden box*) There!

Valerie Fox What is it? The complete works of Jung?

Mrs Fox Here.

She gives the box to Gene as she replies to Valerie.

It would never be Jung, my dear. It would only ever be the works of the Master.

George Fox Christ?

Mrs Fox Freud. (*To Gene.*) Go on. Something from the past. Something extremely dear to you. Something which perhaps may trigger –

Gene has opened the box. A look of abject horror on his face.

See? It's your gun!

Gene lifts the gun from the box into view. Everyone holds their breath. Then Gene, revolted, drops the gun on the bed. Throughout the following, Mrs Fox, who has picked up the gun, tries to force it into his hands. He throws himself around the room to try and get away from her. George is trying to pry the gun off his mother and get between she and Gene. Valerie has become hysterical.

The following four speeches are simultaneous:

Gene No! No! Get it away! Take it away! What kind of person would give another person – I don't want it! I don't want it! Please! No! Get away! Leave me alone!

Mrs Fox (*simultaneously*) But you loved it so. I thought that if you could see it once more. Hold it in your hands. Here! Hold it! Hold it! Just for a moment. Take it in your hands. Take it!

George Fox (*simultaneously*) For heavens sake! Mother, why would you give him his gun? This man has been in an insane asylum! Who knows what he's capable of? What he might do. Mother!

Valerie Fox (*simultaneously*) A gun? A gun! Who would do that? I mean, there's no telling what he might do with it. Shoot himself. Shoot us all. Does she want him to shoot us all? Be careful! Stop!

It all finishes with the piercing 'Stop' from Valerie. She cowers with her hands over her ears for she is certain that the gun is going to go off at any moment killing someone. Preferably her mother-in-law. Gene ends with the gun. He's probably standing on the bed.

Mrs Fox Valerie, please! We have guests! (*To Gene.*) I fail to see what has caused you to behave in such an overexcited fashion. For heaven's sake, all George did was bring you up your silly old gun!

George Fox Yes. Wait! What?

Mrs Fox Please climb down from there this instant. It's very dangerous to be flailing around with firearms while indoors.

Gene But why would you give me a gun?!

Mrs Fox To help, of course.

Gene Help?!

Mrs Fox Tell him, George.

George Fox Tell him what?

Mrs Fox You loved to hunt!

Gene Hunt?

Mrs Fox It started with a Bee-Bee gun we gave you when you were five. A squirrel wasn't it, George?

George Fox Mother, he has a gun.

Mrs Fox Or was it a rabbit?

Gene Rabbit?

Mrs Fox Your first. They're all of them upstairs in the attic.

Gene In the attic?

Mrs Fox Deer and foxes and beavers and ducks and geese and gulls and squirrels and rabbits and a big old daddy elk you bagged that last summer before you –

George Fox Regular zoo up there. Now, why don't you hand me –

Mrs Fox We'll get James to bring them down for you.

Gene God, no!

Mrs Fox You'd position them all around you in this very room like a woodland scene from some Disney cartoon picture movie.

Valerie Fox Only stuffed.

Gene Stuffed?

Valerie Fox (*at the door calling*) For God's sake, James, where are those drinks?

Mrs Fox There was a very good taxidermist in Sag Harbor.

Gene But – I loathe killing of almost any kind. I mean, I'm certain that I do. I mean, I'm pretty certain I do. I mean, I can't even bear to look at a pork chop on a plate!

Mrs Fox I'm sure once we have them all down here and arranged around you once more –

Gene Please, no!

Mrs Fox Just the smaller, less ferociously posed, of course. There's no point overwhelming you with an elk when a charmingly stuffed beaver may do the trick.

Gene (*practically climbing the walls and inadvertently waving the gun*) No, no, no, no, no, no, no! This isn't – This can't – I'm not –

George Fox Watch where you're pointing that –

Valerie Fox (*simultaneously*) Oh, God! He's gonna kill us –

Mrs Fox Not what, dear?

Gene jumps off the bed and, in desperation, with his free hand seizes the framed photograph of the fat baby.

Gene I mean, who is this?

Mrs Fox Why, that's you, dear.

Gene All I see is a fat baby. Who's telling what this child may look like now?

Mrs Fox *You* obviously.

Gene Says you!

Mrs Fox Says everybody. Perhaps we better send for Dr Patchalk.

George Fox Good idea.

Gene No! No doctors! I've had my fill of doctors!

Mrs Fox But it might help, Jack.

Gene Please, will you stop calling me –

Mrs Fox But, it's your name!

Valerie Fox Where is James with those drinks?

Mrs Fox Oh, Valerie! Your brother-in-law has a gun!

George Fox Why don't you pass it here to –

Mrs Fox I have to say I blame the Russians.

George Fox The Russians!?

Mrs Fox He's been brainwashed, clearly. It's what they do, isn't it? Take our poor, innocent young boys and turn them against their own families, their mothers, their country. What else could account for such recalcitrance?

Gene Maybe that's it. Maybe I am – maybe I've been – *God* only knows what I am!

Mrs Fox There's no point in appealing to God, dear, when your own mother is standing right here in front of you telling you you are *Jack Fox*!

Gene Please, please try and understand. For years and years, as I was lying, rotting in that East German prison hospital, eating – I dunno – potato soup with a dessert spoon, or whiling away the hours counting dead flies on the window ledge of my padded cell in New Jersey –

Valerie Fox Of course New Jersey would be lousy with flies.

George Fox Dead ones, no less.

Mrs Fox When you say 'padded', you mean well-upholstered of course?

Gene I would console myself with dreams of the kind of man I might very well turn out to be. A man of great friendliness and affability –

George Fox Huh!

Mrs Fox George!

Gene Perhaps. A man of integrity and honour –

George Fox Huh!

Valerie George!

Gene A man kind and loving to both humans and beasts alike-

George Huh!

Mrs Fox *and* **Valerie Fox** George!

Gene I'd soothe myself with fantasies of his loving family –

Mrs Fox And here we are! Give your brother the gun.

Gene A family that rallied around him in the dark hours before he was sent off to meet his fate.

Mrs Fox What an astute picture he paints.

Gene A fate so mud-drenched and blood-spattered that even now he wakes from hellish nightmares crying for the consolations of his mother.

Mrs Fox Goodness.

Gene A mother who was a model of love and care.

Mrs Fox Of course.

Gene A mother who could take him in and bandage his wounds and kiss his forehead.

Mrs Fox Who is this superwoman?

Gene A mother who, on the night before her youngest son left for the belly of hell –

Mrs Fox Does he mean –

George Fox The war, Mother, the war.

Gene Stayed by his side, perhaps.

Mrs Fox Perhaps.

Gene Held his hand tight.

Mrs Fox Tight as can be.

Gene Prayed prayers, perhaps.

Mrs Fox Goodness. Prayers even.

Gene All for the safe return of her beloved Jack Fox.

Mrs Fox (*heading out*) You have it exactly! Now, let's all head on downstairs and have a nice tall –

Gene And yet –

Mrs Fox There's more?

George Fox There's more.

Valerie Fox Oh, God.

Gene Instead of this dream, this fantasy. I'm brought out here to find –

Mrs Fox What? What have you found?

George Fox I think he's about to tell us, Mother.

Valerie Fox Man the lifeboats.

Gene A man of, frankly, dubious qualities.

Mrs Fox Dubious?

Gene A man who was most probably lecherous and sadistic to the staff.

Valerie Fox Which staff?

Gene As well as to animals.

George Fox Lecherous to animals?

Valerie Fox Which staff?

Mrs Fox He loved animals.

Gene You just told me he'd shoot them and have them stuffed with cotton wool!

Mrs Fox I can assure you, it is a common misconception that animals are cute and cuddly and easy to love. When confronted with the real thing they are most often ferocious, slimy to the touch and badly odorous. You were doing them a service by shooting them, stuffing them and posing them fondly!

Gene A bankrupt then.

Mrs Fox Financially or morally?

Gene Does it matter?

Mrs Fox Of course it matters. Moral bankrupts can be interesting.

Gene Predatory, cunning, deceitful –

Mrs Fox That's quite a list.

Gene And with a mother, I presently discover –

Mrs Fox Just as Freud predicted! It *always* returns to the mother, doesn't it.

George Fox Oh, God.

Gene A mother whose idea of marking the night her youngest son left this house forever to gory manhood in the bunkers and byways of Brittany, was *not* to stay by his side, *not* to hold his hand, *not* to pray prayers –

Mrs Fox I draw the line at group prayer.

Gene But to get together with a gang of her neighbourhood pals and *PLAY CARDS*!

Mrs Fox (*bursting into tears and rushing to George's side*) Oh dear, Georgie! Make him stop! Make him stop! He's saying the most insufferably cruel things to his mother!

George Fox Why don't we take a –

Mrs Fox That's right, Georgie darling! After all these years! As *you* say, better he had *never come back*!

George Fox *I* say?

Gene *You* say?

Mrs Fox I begged him not to think such things, Jack, but you're so naturally cautious, aren't you, Georgie?

George Fox I –

Mrs Fox You just don't like change, do you? So used to life as we live it here in our little private world.

George Fox I –

Mrs Fox (*to George*) *You*, so tortured by your brother.

Gene I, tortured –

Mrs Fox (*reeling on Gene*) Terribly. For years and years. Your cruel little games. And then the ultimate torture.

George Fox Mother!

Valerie Fox (*simultaneously*) God!

Mrs Fox Cruelty like *I* was subjected to just now.

Valerie Fox I think I'm going to be ill.

Mrs Fox That's right, Valerie dear. How ashamed I am for you to see a son treat his mother like this. Jack here seems to find it incredible that the man he believes himself to be could hunt and bait animals. The proof of such pastimes are in the way in which he hunts and baits *me* now. Screaming and yelling and waving a firearm around like he's in some cheap Russian play! (*Reeling on Gene.*) Who knows what it is that you have been led to believe? Have you been appraised of Jack Fox's awful debts? Of his defrauding my most dear and trusted friends in New York City into giving him the money? Leaving us back here to pick up the price tag for his recklessness?

Gene I –

Mrs Fox Perhaps you're right. Perhaps it is a treacherous failing. To be out. 'Playing cards' as you say. On the very night that you were leaving for war. But in my own defence, it was a Thursday night and I had a long-standing arrangement with the Wilders on Shelter Island.

Anyway, it was not cards. Cards makes it sound like it was some tawdry little game like 'Snap'. It was canasta! Canasta! Which means 'basket' in Spanish!

Gene You left him to walk out that front door and go to war without a word!

Mrs Fox Given all that had transpired is it any *wonder* that such a silence had descended between mother and son? Anyway, if you must know, I did attempt to approach him.

George Fox *and* **Valerie Fox** (*simultaneously*) You did?

Gene And?

Mrs Fox He had this look. This tone. Like one of those wild animals of his. He said – He said –

Gene What?

Mrs Fox You said you *hated* me!

Marcee comes barrelling in, followed by De Wit.

Marcee Dupont-Dufort Gene! Oh God, Gene! (*Seeing Mrs Fox*) Oh, Mrs Fox, I'm so sorry.

De Wit Dupont-Dufort Marcee, take it easy will you – Holy –! Who let the crackpot have a gun?!

Mrs Fox Silly old George brought it up here to him.

George Fox But –

De Wit Dupont-Dufort You just keep that thing pointed at the floor. That's all.

Mrs Fox I'm so sorry, Mrs Dupont-Dufort, you seem to have stumbled in on the little bumps that accompany a family reunion. The children vying for the parent's love. The little jealousies and puerile filial rivalries.

De Wit Dupont-Dufort That's brothers, Marcee.

Marcee Dupont-Dufort Thanks, De Wit. I know what 'puerile' means.

Mrs Fox The burden doesn't end when they're grown, you know.

Marcee Dupont-Dufort Yes, well, I'm so sorry, Mrs Fox.

Mrs Fox What for, dear?

Marcee Dupont-Dufort Something awful has happened.

Mrs Fox What?

Marcee Dupont-Dufort I just got a phone call.

Mrs Fox Here? Who would be calling *you* out here?

Valerie Fox Perhaps she has to go rescue another unfortunate mutt?

Marcee Dupont-Dufort It's – The other families.

Mrs Fox Which other?

Marcee Dupont-Dufort The other twenty-two. It's all that woman's fault.

George Fox Mrs Dupont-Dufort, what are you talking about?

Marcee Dupont-Dufort The list. I ran it by that woman.

Valerie Fox Which?

Marcee Dupont-Dufort Liz Smith. The journalist.

De Wit Dupont-Dufort Gossip columnist.

Marcee Dupont-Dufort I ran it by her to get her counsel about his prospective families. It's why we began here. She thought – Well, I'll just come straight out and say it. She thought you were the most well-bred.

Valerie Fox *Inbred* more like.

Mrs Fox Val!

Marcee Dupont-Dufort But she's gone and written an article about it. In the *Times*. Apparently. This morning. We were on the road so early to get to him in Jersey we didn't have time for coffee, let alone the *Times*. Anyway, she's gone and printed all the names! All twenty-two of them! And then that sorry excuse for a butler De Wit has hanging around at our place, back in the city, he answers the phone –

De Wit Dupont-Dufort Don't look at me.

Marcee Dupont-Dufort The fact is, he let it slip to one of the families that we were out here in Amagansett. And, well, he may as well have gone and taken out a full-page advertisement in the *Post*, cos they're on their way. All of them. All twenty-two of them. To claim him as their own!

Juliette rushes in.

Mrs Fox What is it, Juliette?

Juliette I came up to say that those dogs have been sitting down there in that pot so long that they've turned grey and the water's gone red from waiting.

Mrs Fox Vile. Mr and Mrs Dupont-Dufort, I'd say we'd make amends for our little three-ringed circus here by offering you supper, but I'm afraid grey dogs will be a poor –

Gene You're right.

Everyone stops and turns to Gene, who has been standing quietly out of the way, watching the proceedings, gun in hand.

Mrs Fox What was that, dear?

Gene You're right.

Mrs Fox (*laughing self-deprecatingly*) Well, it's good to be right about something at last. (*To Mrs Dupont-Dufort.*)

85

Jack here has been putting me through the most incredible time of it, Mrs Dupont-Dufort.

Gene (*quiet: a realisation*) I do hate you.

Mrs Fox What, dear?

Gene I do *hate* you.

A collective intake of breath.

All Jack!

Gene And, please! Don't ever, ever, ever, ever, ever refer to me by that name again! *I AM NOT JACK FOX!*

He runs into the bathroom, still holding the gun, and slams the door after him.

Mrs Fox Well! There you have it. You see? What more proof do you need? Slamming doors. Just like old times. Jack's back.

James comes to the door.

Yes, James?

Valerie Fox Where are those drinks?

James I'm sorry, ma'am, there's another telephone call for Mrs Dupont-Dufort.

Marcee Dupont-Dufort Good God!

Mrs Fox Another of the horde, perhaps. James, please escort our guests downstairs. Mrs Dupont-Dufort, you may take your telephone call in the hall, then James here will show you to the dining room and get you started. Juliette, please serve the dogs.

Juliette Alright. But don't say you weren't warned about the colour.

Mrs Fox Thank you, Juliette, I shall be down presently.

Juliette leaves.

Marcee Dupont-Dufort Mrs Fox, perhaps before we head down you might allow me –

Mrs Fox Allow you what, dear?

Marcee crosses to the bathroom door and raps on it.

Marcee Dupont-Dufort Hey! You listening to me in there? There's a whole bunch of folks on their way out here with your name on their dance cards. Got it? If I were you I'd be remembering all kinds of nifty things about my idyllic childhood right here in good old Amagansett. You with me? Good. (*Turning back to the room.*) 'Sharper than a serpent's tooth', is what I always say, Mrs Fox.

Mrs Fox A what?

Marcee Dupont-Dufort The ingratitude of children. (*Making her way to the door.*) Look at those storm clouds. You better batten down those hatches. Come on, De Wit.

And on their way out with James.

De Wit Dupont-Dufort What do you know about serpent's teeth, for Christ's sake? Serpents don't have teeth. They have fangs.

Marcee Dupont-Dufort It's Shakespeare, De Wit. We saw it last month at the – You slept through. Oh, never mind.

They're gone.

Valerie Fox One of us should go in.

Mrs Fox (*dark, low*) Leave him!

Valerie Fox But, he has a gun.

Mrs Fox I'm afraid we've depleted Jack's delicate physiognomy. Being the awful monsters we are. Do you know what hearing her son say such a thing does to a mother?

George Fox I'd never say such a thing.

Mrs Fox What?

George Fox To you. I'd never say such a thing.

Mrs Fox (*barely concealing her disappointment*) No. I suppose you wouldn't.

Valerie Fox Surely we should be concerned that he's locked himself in there with a gun, for Christ's sake.

Mrs Fox I think the only creatures who should be concerned, Valerie dear, are any unsuspecting wild life that may be passing the bathroom window. I seem to recall him bagging a duck from there once.

Valerie Fox Well, I for one am concerned.

George Fox Huh!

Valerie Fox I am! He's clearly had an awful shock. He needs comfort. Care. We should be welcoming him with open arms. We thought he was dead, for Christ's sake! How many people get the chance to have people come back from the dead?

Mrs Fox That's just it, dear. Even after all this. He ups and says he isn't Jack Fox. He may be back with us in body, but he's still dead to us in mind. You see what a hateful ideology communism is?

George Fox What's communism got to do with it?

Mrs Fox Not only has it detained a man from his family and force-fed him sauerkraut for fifteen years, but it has deprived him of the memory of a loving mother. A disgrace.

George slaps himself.

Mrs Fox What was that?

George Fox I don't know. A bug I think. They always set on me before it storms. It's the humidity.

Mrs Fox Poor George. Your blood's too sweet. That's your problem. They don't come near me.

Valerie Fox Or me.

Mrs Fox That's the booze, dear.

George slaps himself again.

Mrs Fox No. There's simply nothing for it. It is our patriotic duty to bring him back. To help him see that he does belong here. With us. Especially now that the hideous multitudes are on their way out here clamouring for him.

George Fox I don't see what more we could do for him. The man is staying in his childhood bedroom, for heaven's –

Slap.

Mrs Fox (*to Valerie*) Where Jack is concerned we must *all* lend a hand.

Valerie Fox (*thinking Mrs Fox means the booze*) Alright. I'll stop at this one. It's just so darn hot and close and if I have to listen to that Dupont-Dufort woman go on about abandoned dogs my head's going to –

Mrs Fox Leave the Dupont-Duforts to me. Why don't *you* see to Jack, dear?

George slaps himself.

Valerie Fox What do you mean?

Mrs Fox What might you think I mean, dear?

Valerie Fox (*a desperate look to George*) But, there's a certain –

Mrs Fox Certain what?

Valerie Fox History?

Mrs Fox It seems that *history* is precisely what's called for at the moment. You'd agree with that, wouldn't you, George darling?

George Fox I –

He slaps himself.

Mrs Fox Time is of the essence. We've been given a very slim window. Are we going to let him slip out of it? His head full of the most ludicrous lies about his life here with us? Fantastical stories about the kinds of people we are? The kind of mother I am? Put there by God only knows who. If he leaves in such a state we may never hear from him again. Ever, ever, again. Any of us. We wouldn't want that, would we? Val?

Valerie Fox No.

Mrs Fox Well then –

A slap from George.

We really should be getting down. We're being the most boorish hosts. Come on, George. Let's see if we can get you something for those bugs. We don't want you turning all blotchy over the franks now do we?

She slaps her arm. Regards the carcass plastered thereon. Peels it off and tosses it away.

Well, what do you know.

She goes.

Valerie Fox George, I . . .

A moment between them. Excruciating. Then . . .

George Fox I better go pick out some records to have with the dinner.

He scurries out after his mother. Valerie is left alone in the room. Stands taking a few drags of her cigarette. Thinking. Watching the lightning play out to sea. Far below, in the dining room, André Claveau might be heard singing 'Domino'. Valerie goes to the bathroom door. Then changes her mind. She resolutely butts out her cigarette and crosses the room to leave. Just as she reaches the hallway door a single gunshot from the bathroom.

BANG!

She throws herself back across the room and on to the bathroom door, hammering and yelling and trying to gain access.

Valerie Fox Jack! Oh my God! Jack! Jack, please! Are you alright? Please! Please say something! Jack! Jack! Please, are you –

Suddenly the door opens and a dishevelled Gene appears.

Oh my God, Jack! I thought you'd . . . Thank God. Thank God. Come and sit down. Are you alright? Let me look at you. Are you hurt? Is there blood? Is there bleeding? Let me look! Let me –

Gene I'm alright.

Valerie Fox You're alright.

Gene The gun went off.

Valerie Fox Thank God. Thank God. You're alright.

Gene The thing was loaded.

Valerie Fox I thought you'd –

Gene I was on the bidet.

Valerie Fox I was sure you'd –

Gene Turns out there are very few places to sit in a bathroom that don't encourage thoughts of evacuation. I plumped for the bidet. I must have nodded off with my finger on the trigger. There's a hole clear through the ceiling.

Valerie Fox Never mind about that. The main thing is you're alright. You're alright. Jack darling, you're alright.

Gene Yes. I'm alright, body-wise, but I'm not so sure – Wait!

Valerie Fox What?

Gene 'Darling'?

Valerie Fox (*oh dear*) What are you . . .

Gene You called me –

Valerie Fox No.

Gene Yes.

Valerie Fox No, surely –

Gene You did.

Valerie Fox I was shocked. It was a shock to have that thing go off and to imagine you –

Gene 'Darling'.

Valerie Fox In that moment. I mistook you for – It's a term – Isn't it? Endearment? Affection? 'Darling'. 'Darling'. People say it all the time.

Gene (*backing away from her, from the idea of it all*) You and I –

Valerie Fox You need to get undressed.

Gene You and *he* –

Valerie Fox I mean, out of that robe.

Gene We – They –

Valerie Fox And into something decent.

Gene You and –

Valerie Fox And have a hot dog.

Gene You and Jack Fox –

Valerie Fox Do you like hot dogs?

Gene You were having an affair with Jack Fox!

Valerie is reduced to a kind of groping stammer. Run out of rope, she's dangling precariously.

Valerie Fox I, I, I, I, I . . .

The two regard each other. Mouths open like a couple of confused carp. Then she collapses.

Valerie Fox YES!

Gene Good God!

Valerie Fox You must have known!

Gene I? No! Wait! Did I?

Valerie Fox You must have!

Gene For how long?

Valerie Fox One, maybe two –

Gene 'One maybe two –'?!

Valerie Fox Three maybe.

Gene 'Three'?! 'Maybe'?! You're my brother's wife!

Valerie Fox Oh, for God's sake!

Gene How could you?

Valerie Fox The truth is it was *always* you, Jack darling.

Gene If it was '*always*' me, 'Jack darling', why did you end up marrying George darling?

Valerie Fox I was a girl who worked in an office, for Christ's sake! Do you know how many girls there were like me in the City? Girls who worked in offices? Hundreds! Thousands! Making the trek out here every weekend. I'd already turned down a couple of decent proposals over the water cooler. And you were a baby, so when your brother took an interest – What else was I going to do?

Gene There's usually a page in women's magazines that might have answered that question for you.

Valerie Fox George and I were married, and we moved in here. And in a while he was sent to the Air National Guard Station at Quonset Point like a lot of the older men.

Gene Air National Guard to the rescue!

Valerie Fox So to speak.

Gene And you and I?

Valerie Fox So to speak.

Gene Right under my mother's roof? Did she know?

Valerie Fox If she did it was certainly never mentioned. Until now.

Gene What?

Valerie Fox It was your mother who pressed me to come in here to you.

Gene Good God! In front of George? What kind of woman is she?!

Valerie Fox The kind who is desperate to have her son back by any means, I suppose.

Gene And she would sacrifice the happiness of her other son to do so?

Valerie Fox What about *my* happiness? What about our –

Gene You can't be suggesting we carry on as before?

Valerie Fox No. Of course not.

Gene Good. (*Phew!*)

Valerie Fox Wait!

Gene What?

Valerie Fox Yes.

Gene Yes?

Valerie Fox That's exactly what I'm suggesting.

Gene Good God!

Valerie Fox (*trying to make sense of her feelings, to herself as much as to Gene*) I'm so – When we first got the call. I thought. Well. It's been a long time. Fifteen years. And even seeing you, I was – I thought – But just now. As I saw you with your mother. That look in your eyes. That tone in your voice. I realised –

Gene What?

Valerie Fox I wanted you more than ever, Jack!

Gene This is madness! George –

Valerie Fox Oh, George, George, George. I doubt George'd even notice! He'd have his head in some record player or other! Do you know how long it is since he paid me even the slightest notice?

Gene I'm gonna go mad! Give me a goddamned cigarette!

Valerie Fox (*handing him her pack*) Here.

Gene (*trying to fish a cigarette out*) Do I even smoke?

Valerie Fox We all smoke.

His hands are shaking so badly he can't light the cigarette. Valerie takes charge.

Gimme –

She lights his cigarette for him.

Look at me, Jack.

Gene Oh God.

Valerie Fox Can't you remember anything of the young woman you would swim with right out there on this very beach?

Gene I –

Valerie Fox And play tennis with on that very court?

Gene I –

Valerie Fox Or the woman who would come to you in this very room?

Gene In this very –

Valerie Fox We'd take that old net from the tennis court and rig it up so we could climb out that window and into the branches of the maple and down to the pool and the beach. And walk for miles. We used to say we'd like to walk all night long, all the way along Long Island, right to the East River and then cross the Brooklyn Bridge, plunge into the heart of the City and never be heard from again. Disappear forever. Does none of that –

Gene You might as well be speaking to me in Pekinese.

Valerie Fox Then what about this?

She kisses him hard. He resists. Falls. Resists again. Falls again. Falls hard. Then . . .

Gene Wait! No! This is –

Valerie Fox Do you remember *that* girl?

Gene I have no desire to make love to my brother's wife.

Valerie Fox But you already have.

Gene But, I'm not –

Valerie Fox Yes, yes, We've heard you already. You're not Jack Fox.

Gene I refuse to accept that I engaged in any of this outrageous behaviour.

Valerie Fox But you did do something of the kind just earlier.

Gene What do you mean?

Valerie Fox You spoke to your mother with real hatred. An hour or two with the people from your past and you're back to your old self in no time at all. You simply picked up where you left off, Jack dear. It's who you are. The fact is you're going to have to give up this little fantasy of life as a chump without a past. If you accept me, Jack darling, you might be able to accept yourself. This is who you are.

Gene Is that so?

Valerie Fox Yes.

Gene Well, if this is 'who I am' –

Valerie Fox Yes?

Gene Why don't you go on and tell me this then.

Valerie Fox What?

Gene If this is who I am – who I really and truly am – why does this cigarette make me feel like I'm going to go ahead and loose my *GODDAMNED LUNCH*?!

He throws himself into the bathroom once more and slams the door shut behind him. The sound of him retching.

Valerie takes a moment to compose herself. Lights a cigarette. She approaches the bathroom door.

Valerie Fox Listen, Jack darling. Time is of the essence. There is absolute proof. Proof which only I would –

Gene (*off*) I don't believe it!

Valerie Fox I haven't said anything yet. It will all be much simpler if you just listen to me.

Gene (*off*) I doubt that!

Valerie Fox Believe me. The inheritance I can offer you may seem complicated, but at least it will free you from the approaching hordes of families.

Gene (*off*) I'm not listening!

Valerie Fox If you are who I say you are and our relationship is as I have said it is then I will be in a position to know something about you that nobody else will know.

Gene (*off*) Go away!

Valerie Fox (*deep breath*) There's a scar.

Gene (*off*) I don't have any scars!

Valerie Fox You do. Under your left shoulder blade. Very small. Barely a quarter-inch across.

Gene (*off*) How do you know?

Valerie Fox Because I gave it to you, is how. With a hat pin.

The door to the bathroom slowly opens. Gene is standing there.

Gene A hat pin?

Valerie Fox Who knows? It was all I could lay my hands on at the time.

Gene At what time?

Valerie Fox I was enraged. I thought you'd been with someone. Another woman.

Gene Which woman?

Valerie Fox The maid!

She butts her cigarette. Gulps the dregs of her cocktail. And walks right out of the room.

It's dark now. Flashes of lightning in the brooding sky. The sound of the ocean through the open balcony doors.

Slowly, Gene goes to the mirror in the door of the armoire. He loosens his bathrobe. He turns his back to the mirror, straining to see something there.

He crumples, sobbing quietly to himself. Then louder and louder.

Black.

And Charles Aznavour sings . . . 'For Me . . . Formidable'.

Three

The same young man's bedroom.

The white-hot midday light streams through the open balcony door and on to George, who is sleeping in an armchair or curled up on the bed. Sacha Distel sings 'Ouah! Ouah! Ouah! Ouah!' from a portable record player set up in an improvised fashion somewhere in the room. Arranged around George in charming little groupings, both on chairs and the bed and on the floor, is a collection of stuffed animals. It looks as if the inhabitants of some zoo had been taxidermied and dumped into the room. There's even an elk's head propped up someplace. Cutting a noisy path through the music, a single-engine crop-duster airplane swoops low and loud over the audience's heads and lands on a stretch of lawn on the other side of the pool.

The door to the room flies open and Juliette is there. Expectantly she scans the room, regards George sleeping and leaves, closing the door behind her.

A pair of hands become visible gripping the balcony rail. A figure hauls itself up and over and comes crashing down on to the balcony. It's Gene, of course. He is taking particular pains not to be seen by anyone down below. Frankly, he looks pretty haggard. He's managed to pull together an outfit of badly fitting trousers and a shirt, but as he's been out all night in the storm he looks a little like Robinson Crusoe. Perhaps he's wrapped in an old tennis net which he's used to get himself into the maple tree and up and over the balcony. Once he's in the room and extricated from the tennis net he notices the animals. He starts at the sight of a particularly incredible-looking beaver. He backs into the portable record player sending the needle scratching across the surface of the record, silencing it and waking George.

Gene Holy cow! What the . . .

George Fox (*simultaneously*) *What!* Oh, it's you.

George Fox I must have – What's the time?

Gene I dunno. Noon?

George Fox How did you –

Gene The maple tree. Seemed like the only way to get back up here without being accosted by what looks like the Long Island branch of the Mormon Tabernacle Choir down there.

George Fox The place is crawling.

Gene My prospective families, no doubt.

George Fox Mother's corralled most of them in the pool house, I think. James has orders to keep the gin flowing and Juliette is up to her elbows in cold potato salad. It's hoped that the combination of starch and alcohol will keep them drunk, drowsy and docile for at least the time being.

Gene And you thought you'd –

George Fox Only place to get any peace.

Gene (*referring to the stuffed animals*) What? You and the cast of *Bambi* here?

George Fox Mother thought it might help.

Gene I bet she did. What is that?

George Fox That? That's an elk, I believe.

Gene An elk.

George Fox I believe so.

Gene That elk looks about how I feel.

He heads for the bathroom.

George Fox (*calling in to him*) It was *some* storm.

Gene (*off*) Shoulda been out in it.

George Fox We thought you might have been hit by lightning or something.

Gene pokes his head through the open door. His shirt open, a towel over his shoulder and lathering a brush preparing to shave.

Gene Thought, or wished?

George Fox We were worried. To see you fly downstairs and tear straight on out into the rain like that. I thought Dupont-Dufort was going to choke on her hot dog.

Gene (*off*) I needed some air.

George Fox Boy did you get it, and how.

Gene (*off*) This house has a way of feeling about an inch big.

George Fox I never noticed.

Gene (*off*) I just had to break out somehow. (*Coming in. Face lathered.*) Don't you ever feel like you wanna, wanna –

George Fox Wanna what?

Gene Come on, would ya! Sitting there all nice and – I dunno, with your fancy French records and the rest of it. Let's call it like it is?

George Fox How would that be, then?

Gene If Jack Fox were my kid brother and I was you I'd give him about a ten-second head start and go after him with that gun like he was one of his precious badgers or bunnies or whatever.

He goes into the bathroom.

George Fox I don't know what you're talking about.

Gene comes straight back out, razor in hand.

Gene For Pete's sake! He was being fast with your wife! And you just – what – (*Mimicking him.*) 'Oh, don't worry about that. Here. You want me to put a little Charley Aznavour on the record player so that you two kids can go ahead and slow dance?'

George Fox Don't.

Gene (*breaking into an absurd waltz back into the bathroom*) A one, two, three. A one, two, three –

George Fox Don't.

Gene (*off*) A one, two, three. A one, two –

George launches himself from his chair, across the room and into the bathroom. We hear the sound of a strangulated protest, and something fly off a counter and smash on a tiled floor and two grown men wrestling. Before long Gene and George fly out of the bathroom. George has hold of Gene around the collar. Shaving foam everywhere.

Gene Attaboy!

George Fox I should hate you!

Gene Yes, you should! Well, him!

George Fox You wanna know the truth?

Gene Why not.

George Fox I was waiting up here.

Gene For what?

George Fox For you.

Gene I'm flattered.

George Fox All these years I dreamed about what I would do –

Gene Do it!

George Fox Say –

Gene Say it!

George Fox If I ever got half a chance –

Gene Now you got it!

George Fox And now you're here –

Gene I am! He is!

George Fox And I've got all of this inside of me. Ready to –

Gene Yes!?

George Fox I'm gonna –

Gene Yes!?

George Fox I'm just gonna –

Gene Let him have it!

> *George drops him like a hot brick. And, referring to the shaving foam on his face:*

George Fox *WIPE YOUR GODDAMN FACE, WHY DON'T CHA!*

Gene (*hounding him, trying to get him to take a 'pop'*) Wait! What about all that stuff inside of you?

George Fox It's no use.

Gene For God's sake! You're no better than one of these stuffed rodents here! Think of your *wife*!

George Fox Huh!

Gene Think of me. Him. His hands all over her. His hideous breath at her throat. His lips on hers. You should take that gun and put him out of your misery. Nobody would blame you. *I* wouldn't blame you. And I'd be dead!

George Fox I can't!

Gene Why not?

George Fox It's not as simple as that.

Gene Oh, yeah? Cos it seems pretty goddamned simple to me.

George Fox Ever since you arrived. Ever since I saw you. Skulking around the pool like some kinda bizarre ghost or something. I've been setting myself up to take a pop.

Gene And I'm saying 'pop' away!

George Fox But then I see you. Up close. I talk to you and –

Gene What?

George Fox There's something about your face.

Gene My face? (*The shaving cream.*) Well, of course, right now . . .

He heads for the bathroom.

George Fox I see *him.*

Gene (*off*) Wretched.

George Fox That morning he marched off along the drive there with his kitbag.

Gene (*off*) Weasel.

George Fox Or years before that, laughing and playing with him in the pool.

Gene (*off*) Mean little –

George Fox Or the day, long before that, when we first put that Bee-Bee gun in his hand.

Gene (*off*) Contemptible.

George Fox Or the evenings he'd sit on the beach and listen to us tell tales of the father he never really knew.

Gene (*off*) Wretched, weaselly, mean, contemptible –

George Fox Listen. I know I may seem like some kinda – I know what people think of me. Moping around here all these years with my head stuck in a record player listening to all this continental stuff like God only knows what. 'Oh, that George is harmless alright. Bit of an odd-ball maybe, but if a hankering for Frenchified music is the worst you can say about a fella, then he's not half bad.'

Gene (*off*) Half bad's better than *all* bad.

George Fox But that's the thing.

Gene (*off*) What thing?

George Fox What people don't understand. I'm not just that. 'Harmless ole George'. Truth is, I knew what was up. Truth is, I knew it almost before you did.

Gene (*coming in, his face partly shaved*) What do you mean?

George Fox You were always out there in the world. Doing things. Messing stuff up.

Gene A bum.

George Fox Yes. But also a kinda free bum. I envied you for it. Terribly. So, when Val came out here with all the other girls from the city, and I saw you strike up a – I was never really that interested in her. I just – It was the first thing that I'd seen you want. Really want. Badly. The first thing that I could prevent you from getting by taking it for myself. I knew at the end of the day, given her situation, that she'd plump for the older brother rather than the younger. I *knew* what I was doing. But I went ahead and did it because I knew that it'd take something from you that you really, truly wanted.

Gene Except Jack Fox went ahead and took it anyway.

George Fox But if I hadn't taken it in the first place –

James comes in.

James Sorry to disturb you, gentlemen, but all hell's breaking loose down there.

George Fox What do you mean?

James More of Captain Fox's families have turned up. Another few were on the first train from Penn Station. There's even a couple of them arrived in an airplane.

George Fox An airplane?

James Little crop-duster. Landed it right in the front garden between Mrs Fox's euphorbia and her coreopsis.

Gene Tight squeeze, no doubt.

James Mrs Dupont-Dufort says you better get yourself dressed and down there to the pool house before there's some kinda riot. (*Busying himself at the armoire.*) I'm thinking you'll need a suit, sir.

Gene I better – (*His half-shaven face.*) Can't go to a firing squad in a pool house with a half-shaven face.

George Fox I'll go down and see what I can do.

Gene makes to go into the bathroom.

Hey.

Gene What?

George Fox You could do yourself a favour.

Gene What's that?

George Fox Forgive him. He was a kid. That's what I'm talking about. When I look at you. I see it. He was just a kid.

He goes.

Gene (*as he regards the stuffed elk's head*) Why would anyone in the world want to –

He heads for the bathroom.

James (*a pair of trousers*) Give these a try, sir.

Gene takes the pants as he passes and goes into the bathroom.

Gene (*referring to the stuffed elk's head*) You know I saw one, James.

James One?

Gene (*off*) Of those. Last night. When I ran out into the storm.

James Crazy.

Gene (*off*) In that grove of pines that skirt the dunes.

James Better check yourself for ticks. End up with that Lyme disease, you know.

Gene (*comes in shaven, climbing into his trousers*) We stood there. In the rain. Just. Looking at one other. He was redder than that one. But the eyes. Even in the dark and the rain.

James gives him a shirt.

Thanks. You know, they can stuff these things with as much cotton wool or whatever it is that they like. Put glass marbles in their heads for eyes. But there's no way they can ever pass for the real thing. It's the eyes. Something. Behind them. Something true. These things are just death. Pretending to be life.

James (*shoes*) Death got no business pretending to be life, Captain, sir. You go ahead and try these.

Gene (*trying on shoes*) Maybe that's what I've gotta do. Be like one of these stuffed fur coats. (*The animals.*) Dead. Faking being real. Faking being Jack Fox. What else can I do? Go back to New Jersey?

Shoes on.

James Wouldn't advise that, sir. (*Helping him on with a jacket.*) Try this.

Gene (*the suit fits him perfectly*) Pass muster?

James Good as we gonna get, sir.

Gene Captain Jack Fox resurrected from the grave and reporting for duty! Stuffed! Let's get this over with. (*His forced smile cracks.*) God, a whole lifetime of –

James You alright there, sir?

Gene Once I go down there to the pool house and announce that I am, in fact, Jack Fox, there's no turning back, is there?

James Don't believe there is, sir, no.

Gene Here I go then.

He goes to leave.

James Wait a minute.

Gene What is it?

James just looks at him.

What?

James I'm gonna tell you something now. I'm gonna tell it once. I shouldn't. But I'm gonna. So you better listen up.

Gene James, I really have to get down to the –

James I was looking at all these old suits you got hanging in here.

Gene Take your pick.

James I got myself two. That's enough. One's for Sundays. The other's for burying me in.

Gene You have a suit for that?

James Sure do. Along with a special account to pay for the funeral.

Gene I'm sure this is fascinating, James, but under the circumstances –

James These suits got me to thinking of my funeral suit.

Gene Charming.

James It's a nice old suit came to me from my daddy. He got it from a friend of his. From the South. This friend didn't need it any more cos he was dead.

Gene Presumably he wasn't buried in it.

James He didn't get buried.

Gene Cremated?

James There were a few fellas. This fella was one of them. They worked for people. Not treated well. Like *really* not treated well. Do you understand what I'm saying to you?

Gene I understand.

James So, these fellas would stage their own death. A fire or something. Everything burned up. No trace. And they'd vanish. Into thin air. Poof!

The two men look at one another.

Valerie Fox (*a long way off*) James?!

Gene What are you suggesting?

Valerie Fox (*a long way off*) James?! Are you up there?

James They had to kill themselves in order to live.

Valerie Fox (*off*) James?! Are you listening?!

Gene But if I were to kill off poor old Jack Fox in some French field someplace –

Valerie Fox (*off*) James?! I'm coming up!

Gene Who would that leave me to be?

James That's up to you. Some people even say it's what America is for. Make yourself whatever you want. For certain, lucky people, that is.

Valerie comes in.

Valerie Fox For goodness sake, James! I've been yelling myself hoarse!

James Sorry, ma'am.

Valerie Fox We're all waiting downstairs and I've just seen George and –

James We was just coming, ma'am.

Valerie Fox Having me screaming my lungs out and climbing up and down stairs like a fireman. Honestly, James.

James Yes, ma'am. Sorry, ma'am.

Valerie Fox You go down now and tell them that Captain Fox and I are on our way down.

James Surely, ma'am.

Gene Thank you, James.

James nods at Gene and leaves.

Valerie Fox Honestly, if that man hadn't been in this house for so long –

She is stopped in her tracks by his grin.

Gene Restful night?

Valerie Fox (*wary*) Yes, yes, I suppose so.

Gene And breakfast this morning?

Valerie Fox Yes. Coffee. Breakfast. I guess.

Gene Delightful. Plans for the day?

Valerie Fox For heaven's sake! Would you stop! I've been waiting all morning.

Gene Waiting?

Valerie Fox You must have said something to George just now. I understand that. It's only right that you should broach this whole awful business with him first. The kindest thing to do, after all. And when I saw him just now, and he didn't say anything I thought, I thought, well, you'll want to tell me yourself, of course.

Gene Tell you what?

Valerie Fox What you saw.

Gene Where?

Valerie Fox On your back, for heaven's – Oh, Jack, I'm so, so –

Gene Nothing.

Valerie Fox What?

Gene I saw nothing.

Valerie Fox You saw . . .

Gene That's right. Nothing.

Valerie Fox But, the scar.

Gene I looked for it. But there was nothing there.

Valerie Fox (*low and cold*) What do you mean?

Gene I looked very carefully at my back. There was no scar. You must have been mistaken.

A long moment of disbelief, then . . . she launches herself at him. Gene extricates himself.

Valerie Fox What do you mean? How could you be so . . . I don't understand. Let me see. Let me see!

Gene (*simultaneously*) Just – take it easy. Calm down. Will you please . . . I think you'll find *it's better that way*!

Valerie Fox Better? Better? For *you*, perhaps. Don't you think that what you're about to do has any bearing on anyone else? For Christ's sake, Jack. You're going to deny your family? Your home? Yourself?

Gene That's exactly what I plan to do. The fact is. I don't like you very much. Or your mother-in-law or poor Jack Fox for that matter. If I refuse to own you, you can never own me.

Valerie Fox And your love for me? What are you going to do with that? Deny that as well? Just go on and pretend that it was nothing?

Gene That's exactly what I plan to do.

Valerie Fox How can you just turn it off like water from a faucet?

Gene Because it's as if you were telling me about, I dunno, a town in – what? Japan?

Valerie Fox Japan?!

Gene Your love is like a town I've never been to. Oh, I can appreciate what you're saying to me alright; that the town exists, that it may even be quite pretty – green, temples, Buddhist monks, that kinda thing – but as I've never been there I have no real understanding of the place you're describing. Your love is like that to me. A foreign land.

Valerie Fox Then I will tell the others.

Gene What will you tell them?

Valerie Fox About the scar. That I know about the scar. That I've seen the scar. That I gave you the scar.

Gene And risk the kind of attention that might bring?

Valerie Fox Look at you!

Gene What?

Valerie Fox In trying to divorce yourself from us. From me. You've proven once and for all that you are, in fact, Jack Fox.

Gene How so?

Valerie Fox You're enjoying yourself. Gratifying, is it? To refuse me? To make a fool out of me?

Gene (*a little chastened*) I . . . (*Faltering.*) No. I don't believe I . . .

  Juliette comes in.

Valerie Fox What is it?

Juliette Sorry to interrupt. (*She beams at Gene.*) Mrs Dupont-Dufort sent me up to ask that you hurry as quickly as you can. They're waiting for you in the pool house. Your other families are beginning – Well, Mrs Dupont-Dufort believes that unless you come down pretty soon there's going to be some kinda 'insurrection'.

Gene An insurrection!

Juliette That's what she said.

Valerie Fox Well, you tell Mrs Dupont-Dufort that we're on our way down.

Juliette Of course.

Juliette stares at Gene. She very badly wants to say something to him. Valerie notices she's still in the room.

Valerie Fox Is everything alright, Juliette?

Juliette Sure is.

Valerie Fox You heard me then. Go and tell Mrs Dupont-Dufort that Captain Fox is on his way.

Juliette Alright.

She goes.

Valerie Fox Off you go then! What are you waiting for?

Gene What do you mean?

Valerie Fox The other families. Your other families. You seem to have forgotten.

Gene No, I –

Valerie Fox Yes? If you're not going to choose us, Jack. You are going to have to choose one of them. At least there's plenty to choose from. Twenty-two, did Mrs Dupont-Dufort say? Just think of them all now. Down there. In the pool house. We never sought you out, you see. But they? They come like rabid dogs. Hungry for their little Tom, Dick or Harry. My, there will be some road worker from Jersey Heights whose boy they thought lost in France. 'Where is France exactly, by the way?' they'll ask. 'That's the one right next to Greece, ain't it?' 'What does it matter now that you're home,

Garfield.' 'Here. Let us show you to your room. It's a little small. We had it turned into a bedroom for your Aunt Bertha from Buffalo. You don't mind sharing with Bertha, do you?' Or, or, or . . . Gideon, who runs a diner in Yonkers. He'll be beside himself at the prospect that his little Herschel has returned home from the war and can take over from him working in the diner. He doesn't really need any help on the floor of the restaurant. Oh, no! He's got your five sisters for that. It's the fryer he wants help with. The deep fryer in the kitchen. You see, he's getting too old now to lift the potatoes in and out. Only a couple hundred a day. Pounds that is.

Gene That's –

Valerie Fox Or then, the ageing couple from West Virginia. What a razz that'll be. No one to work their little godforsaken plot of earth way up in the mountains. But not now! Now? Well their little Harlan has returned to them, hasn't he? And they've got a nice girl picked out for him. A nice homey girl from the local church. She's your cousin. 'But you don't mind about that, do you Harlan? After all your momma and papa were brother and sister and it hasn't hurt us none.'

Gene You're –

Valerie Fox Go on! Go to your families!

Manhandling him and continuing directly on . . .

As you don't want us, you better go choose one of them, then. Go on! What are you waiting for? Tick-tock, tick-tock! Crowded down there in the pool house. Guzzling all the free liquor they can and smacking their hideous chops to get their awful, hardened paws on their little piece of whatever your name is . . .

Gene (*simultaneously*) Stop it, stop it, stop it! Don't push me! I'll go in my good time. Would you stop it with all this talk? This hideous awful talk. No wonder I can't find it in my heart to love you. No wonder there's no memory of you left inside my thick skull. You'd drive a normal man to amnesia just so he could forget the sound of your voice!

Valerie Fox (*continuing on*) . . . *OH, WE'RE GOING TO SEEM LIKE A GODDAMN PICNIC NEXT TO THEM!*

Gene I'm not going!

Valerie Fox What do you mean to do, then?

Gene I'm, I'm, I'm going away!

Valerie Fox Where, for heaven's sake?

Gene I don't know. It doesn't matter.

Valerie Fox Only a child talks like that. I'm sure if you asked my mother-in-law's goddamned shrink she'd tell you. Grown-ups know that they must choose a destination when they travel. Where's it gonna be? Buffalo? Des Moines? Of course if you had money that would be a different thing altogether, but –

Gene I'll walk!

Valerie Fox You will, will you? Where to?

Gene Across the fields. To, to, to – I don't know. Into Sag Harbor and then over to Shelter Island and on to the North Fork and –

Valerie Fox Be picked up by the police as some kinda vagrant or something? An escaped lunatic wandering around in the Hamptons? You know what people are like out here? The very fact that you're walking and not in a car will raise suspicions. Nobody walks here. Why do you think there are no sidewalks, for God's sake?

Gene I'll run!

Valerie Fox And the police will come even faster. I can see it now. 'MAN SEEN RUNNING IN THE HAMPTONS!'

Gene There's the asylum. I could –

Valerie Fox Terrific! I'll drive you back there myself, shall I? It's my patriotic duty, after all. Tell them that the terrible communists clearly did a number on you. 'Sure, he's been brainwashed,' I'll say. 'So sad. Can't even recall his loving all-American family.' They'd *love* that, wouldn't they? Sure, they'd have some delightful means of washing all that hateful socialistic ideology right outta that brain of yours.

Gene I could take you in my bare hands and –

Valerie Fox What?

Gene Wrap them around your throat so tight –

Valerie Fox Even if you killed me you'd be found. You can't escape from the whole world, Jack. Whether you want it or not, you must belong to someone.

Gene I could – I could – I could –

That's it. He's spent. He sinks on to the bed.

Valerie Fox (*stroking his hair*) Darling. Darling Jack. I'm so sorry to have to perform this, kind of, shock therapy on you. Don't you see? Without us, you're nothing. What is it you said? A goldfish in a bowl. With only a minute's worth of memory to cling to. (*Setting herself to rights.*) Listen. Listen to me. You dry your eyes and get yourself together. I'm going to go down to the pool house. I'll calm things down a little. Then. When you can. You come down and let the families know what you have discovered.

Gene What have I discovered?

Valerie Fox That you have found a scar. A scar on your back. That that scar has awakened in you the knowledge of your true identity. That you are in fact Captain Jack Fox. And that you're home.

She kisses him lightly on top of the head and leaves.
Devastated by her onslaught, he takes off one of his shoes and hurls it at the armoire. The mirror in the front shatters. He sits, his head in his hands. Slowly the door of the armoire opens and a small boy dressed as an aviator climbs out. Gene stares at the child. There is no shock here. 'Of course,' he thinks. 'I have simply gone mad.'

Small Boy (*regarding the broken glass*) That's seven years' bad luck.

Gene Only seven?

The Small Boy crosses the room to head out.

Can I help you?

Small Boy I don't think so.

Gene Wait. What were you doing in my armoire?

Small Boy I was looking for some peace and quiet.

Gene You find any?

Small Boy Until you started shouting.

Gene Sorry about that.

The Small Boy is at the door.

Wait. I understand the 'what'. But, *how* did you get into my armoire?

Small Boy I opened the door and climbed in.

Gene *When*, then?

Small Boy Before. There was a lot of carry-on downstairs and I slipped away to look for some peace and quiet and I came in here. And then someone was coming and I climbed into the armoire.

Gene Do you climb into armoires often?

Small Boy If I'm in need of peace and quiet.

Gene Perhaps that's what I should do.

Small Boy Now that would be silly.

Gene How so?

Small Boy You ever seen a grown-up sitting in an armoire?

Gene I don't suppose I have. Listen, where are your parents anyway?

Small Boy Dead.

Gene Sorry for your loss.

Small Boy They died in a plane crash. I was a baby. They found me in the wreckage wedged between an inflatable life raft and ten back issues of *Time* magazine.

Gene Awful.

Small Boy I don't remember a thing. My mother and father were visiting my mother's parents who lived out here on Long Island. And my papa was flying my momma and me back to our home in California.

Gene Your father was –?

Small Boy He was a pilot. But not a good enough one, I guess. He hit a patch of bad weather over Great Bend, Kansas, and we crash-landed in a field. Everyone got killed.

Gene Well, I'll be –

Small Boy Except for me.

Gene All thanks to *Time* magazine. Remind me to take out a subscription. So you're an orphan?

Small Boy That's right.

Gene So am I. Sort of. And, you're here with your . . .

Small Boy Uncle Job. We flew over last night.

Gene You take the red-eye?

Small Boy No. We got a plane. A little one. For dusting crops. We left like a rocket as soon as we heard.

Gene As soon as you heard, what?

Small Boy They've got this guy here.

Gene Which guy?

Small Boy A guy who's been lost for years in Picatinny, New Jersey. It turns out that this fella –

Gene Turns out that this fella might be related to Uncle Job somehow. A long-lost nephew or something, and soon as you heard about it you and Uncle Job hot-footed it over here to the other side of the country in a single-engine crop-duster to see if he belongs to you and if you can take him back to California with you. Well, you should go right on down and tell Uncle Job that he shouldn't have wasted his time and airplane gas.

Small Boy Why?

Gene Because there's little chance that the nephew, or whatever he is, will recognise Uncle Job.

Small Boy There's no reason he should. You're right on one thing. It is a nephew we're looking for. But you're wrong on the other. It's not Uncle Job who's doing the looking.

Gene What do you mean?

Small Boy Uncle Job isn't the uncle. I am.

Gene What do you mean?

Small Boy It's kinda screwy, but the way it works is that my grandfather had kids when he was very old to a girl who was very young. Uncle Job says it happens like that sometimes on account of something called 'excessive libido'. Anyway, I was born twenty-six years after my grandfather's kid. This fella who's been lost in Picatinny, New Jersey, is *my* nephew. *I'm* the uncle. Probably.

Gene But this Uncle Job –

Small Boy He's not really my uncle. He's an old flying buddy of my father's from the war. When my parents got killed, Uncle Job moved in to the family farm in California to take care of me.

Gene So it's just you and Uncle Job on this little ole family farm in California? What do you need to come on this goose chase for this fella from Picatinny, New Jersey, for? Why not just leave the pathetic creature be?

Small Boy It's because of the oil.

Gene I see. Oil?

Small Boy The oil on the farm.

Gene The oil on the farm.

Small Boy Our farm, yes. Uncle Job says there's a fair amount of it.

Gene And by 'fair amount' he means . . .

Small Boy Uncle Job says there's enough oil on our farm to power a city.

Gene How big a city?

Small Boy Chicago.

Gene Go on.

Small Boy Uncle Job says first we gotta put in pumps.

Gene So, put in the pumps.

Small Boy Uncle Job says my parents' will states that I can't raise a finger on the property until I'm twenty-one. Uncle Job says that eleven years is a long time to wait when there's enough oil sitting under the ground to power a city.

Gene Specially if that city's Chicago.

Small Boy But, Uncle Job says that my parents' will says that if we were to locate a living relative before I got to be twenty-one, that that relative would have the right to manage my affairs –

Gene Managing your affairs presumably means putting in a great big pump to pump oil. Good ole Uncle Job must be very eager to find your nephew.

The door opens. It's De Wit Dupont-Dufort.

De Wit Dupont-Dufort What the heck's going on in here?

Gene I'm making friends.

De Wit Dupont-Dufort Who with – Oh! You with the families?

Gene He's with the families.

De Wit Dupont-Dufort Then you better scram back down to the pool house. They're starting to serve lunch. It's cold potato salad. You like cold potato salad?

The Small Boy shakes his head.

Gene He wanted some peace and quiet.

De Wit Dupont-Dufort Let me tell you this. You're in the wrong place for peace and quiet, my short friend. I've been looking for it this past forty-eight hours and I've come to the conclusion there's none to be found out here.

Gene You may wanna try the armoire.

De Wit Dupont-Dufort Are you drunk?

Gene No.

De Wit Dupont-Dufort Just plain crazy, huh? Now listen. I've been sent up here by the women to get you downstairs. They told me that if I don't have you with me when I come down those stairs that it'll cost me more than my life's worth. I'm not one hundred per cent sure what's more than my life's worth, but I'm not prepared to take the risk and find out. So, I'm asking you now, nicely, to do me a favour. You come down those stairs with me and go out into that pool house and have a plate of cold potato salad and maybe a highball or two for courage and then you clear your throat and tap a spoon or something against your glass to get everybody's attention and you make a nice little speech. You thank everybody for coming. (*To the Small Boy.*) You always thank everybody for coming. (*Back to Gene.*) And you say that you're sorry to have caused such a ruckus but just now as you were taking your bath you reached for the soap and it came to you in a blinding flash. You are Jack Fox of Amagansett, Long Island, and you're pleased to say that you belong here with these crazy sons-of-bitches – (*To the Small Boy.*) You never heard that. (*Back to Gene.*) And in saying so you will disabuse that small league of nations they got gathering down there that you are in any way kin to them or theirs and then we can all get the hell – (*To the Small Boy.*) You never heard that. (*Back to Gene.*) Outta here and go home. There's a poker game in the city at the Roses Club starts at nine. If we leave in half an hour I can make it back for that. You got me? (*To the Small Boy.*) You play poker?

   The Small Boy shakes his head.

If you take my advice you'll learn. Makes life liveable.

That and cigars. Start smoking at your first opportunity. (*To Gene.*) You still here?

Gene Mr Dupont-Dufort, the way things are going I might as well blow my brains out with that gun in there right now.

De Wit Dupont-Dufort Take it easy in front of the short guy.

Gene I'm sorry, but I'm desperate. If I go down those stairs now, I can't guarantee what might happen.

De Wit Dupont-Dufort I see. Firstly, who is this?

Gene What?

De Wit Dupont-Dufort This. Short person. Who is he? Who are you, sir?

Gene He's looking for his nephew.

De Wit Dupont-Dufort His nephew must be exceedingly young.

Gene By a trick of birth and his grandfather's excessive libido and taste for younger women, this young man's nephew is twenty-six years his senior. He has neither mother nor father and he and his Uncle Job, uncle by name you understand, not nature, flew all night in a single-engine crop-duster from their farm in California to meet that fella from Picatinny, New Jersey, to see if it's this young man's long-lost nephew, and if it is, take him back to California with them in their single-engine crop-dusting airplane. Is that about right?

The Small Boy nods his head.

De Wit Dupont-Dufort You impressed me. So listen. (*To the Small Boy.*) Why don't you go on in there and wash your hands. You don't want to get aviation grease on that potato salad now, do you?

The Small Boy looks at Gene.

Gene The bathroom's through there.

The Small Boy goes.

De Wit Dupont-Dufort I need you to understand that I don't like you.

Gene Oh.

De Wit Dupont-Dufort You've taken up a good part of my wife's attention over the past months. I would ordinarily say that that is a good thing. Only you've taken up the *good* part of my wife's attention. You understand me?

Gene I – No.

De Wit Dupont-Dufort There are certain rights that a husband can expect to enjoy when one is married. It really is the only point of marriage in the first place. That what in single life costs a man candy and corsages and compliments becomes, in married life, a regularly expectable event. Like washing the dog or defrosting the refrigerator or putting out the trash.

Gene I still don't –

De Wit Dupont-Dufort As a single man I'd either have to put the trash out myself or spend a lot of effort, time and money convincing some sweet kid to put the trash out for me. You . . .

Gene I see!

De Wit Dupont-Dufort A married man can expect that at least one quarter of the time his wife will put the trash out.

Gene I see.

De Wit Dupont-Dufort Since she has met you, Mr – Mr whatever-your-name-is, my wife has flatly refused to put

the trash out. The trash is building up. You with me? I got
trash all over the place. Trash that needs to be removed.
Now, I'm not a philandering man. Not a man who might
cajole some other sweet thing to remove the trash for me,
or, worse still, pay to have the trash removed. I'm a
Floridian. That brings with it certain niceties of habit
which I'm sure Yankees find downright old fashioned.
Still, it's what I am and I have no intention of acting
otherwise. The point is, the sooner I find an answer to
the question of *you*, the sooner I get my wife to take the
trash out.

Gene I see.

De Wit Dupont-Dufort No, you don't. Clearly. It seems
to me that if these people here don't suit you as a
prospective family you may want to look west.

Gene West?

De Wit Dupont-Dufort California, for instance?

Gene Calif—

De Wit Dupont-Dufort You always did seem like you
had a touch of lousy Californian in you. You'd fit right
in.

Gene You're suggesting I –

De Wit Dupont-Dufort There may be something. Some
point of reference from your past. Something you *do*
remember. Something which only a *Californian* might
know.

Gene Some –

De Wit Dupont-Dufort You got an unfortunate habit of
not finishing your sentences.

Gene I –

De Wit Dupont-Dufort There you go. You gotta finish a sentence or two. Why not start by talking to that short fella's uncle. Who knows? They might be pleased to hear from you.

Gene I – Of course! I'll – Of course! Wait!

De Wit Dupont-Dufort There's no time for waiting.

The Small Boy comes back in the room.

De Wit Dupont-Dufort You all washed up?

The Small Boy nods.

Will you do something for me?

The Small Boy nods.

Will you take this gentleman here and introduce him to your uncle for me? They got a thing or two they need to talk about. (*To Gene.*) I'll wrangle the rest of them while you're gone. The place is lousy with deadbeats. Let's meet up here. Alright?

The Small Boy takes Gene by the hand and begins to lead him out of the room.

Gene But this is going to be very disappointing for your wife, Mr Dupont-Dufort. She kind of had her heart set on me being Jack Fox.

De Wit Dupont-Dufort You're not understanding here. I loathe my wife. The pleasure I'll derive watching her little plans to dominate in the mansions of the Upper East Side fly out the window and off to California will be worth the cost of the earful I'm gonna get all the way back along the Long Island Expressway.

Gene But the trash?

De Wit Dupont-Dufort I like the trash to be taken out. Doesn't mean I care for the company of the trash collector.

Gene and the Small Boy leave.

*De Wit takes out a cigar. Lights it. Presses the buzzer.
Remembers. 'Shoot.' Goes to go into the hallway to
call James and is met by Juliette in her coat and with
a suitcase heading into the room.*
    *Juliette walks straight by him and into the bathroom
and straight out again. As she does so:*

Perfect timing. You wanna go round up Mrs Dupont-
Dufort and the Foxes and have them come on up here for
me? Oh, and maybe get James to bring up a pitcher of
martinis while you're at it? Dry. Very dry. You lost
something?

A small herd of rhinoceroses are heard in the corridor.

Juliette Where is he?

De Wit Dupont-Dufort Who? Oh. He's having a parley
with a couple o' Californians. (*Noticing the suitcase.*)
You going someplace?

Juliette I'm –

*The aforementioned rhinoceroses muscle their way
into the room expectantly. It's Valerie, George, Marcee
Dupont-Dufort and Mrs Fox.*
    *Seeing Gene is not in the room, Valerie goes straight
into the bathroom and comes straight out again.*

Valerie Jack? Jack? Is he – Where is he? What's
happened? Is he alright?

Marcee Dupont-Dufort De Wit, I thought I told you to
bring him out to the pool house. And don't smoke that
in here.

De Wit Dupont-Dufort Oh, I don't think anyone will
mind if I have a little puff of a celebratory cigar, Marcee.

Mrs Fox Mr Dupont-Dufort, you can puff on a hookah
for all I care as long as you've managed to convince Jack –

Marcee Dupont-Dufort What do you mean, 'celebratory'?

Valerie Fox For God's sake, where is he?

George Fox Calm down, Val.

Valerie Fox No, *you* calm down.

De Wit Dupont-Dufort I believe he had to see a man about a dog.

Valerie Fox What is it with you people and dogs? Juliette, go and tell Captain Fox to come up here this instant.

De Wit Dupont-Dufort And don't forget that pitcher of martinis.

Mrs Fox (*noticing Juliette for the first time*) What on earth are you doing with that suitcase, Juliette?

Juliette Which?

Mrs Fox The one in your hands.

Juliette It's – It's – I'll go get Captain Fox.

She goes.

De Wit Dupont-Dufort (*calling after her*) And that pitcher of martinis.

Mrs Fox Lord knows what's gotten into her.

George Fox (*at the record player*) Why don't I put a little something on while we wait?

Valerie Fox You play your little songs to your heart's content, George. I don't believe there's a thing that you could do today that would unnerve or disgust me.

George Fox If you can think of something do let me know.

Marcee Dupont-Dufort No, really. What do you mean, 'celebratory', De Wit?

Valerie Fox I can't bear this. I'm going to go down and –

De Wit Dupont-Dufort He did say he'd like you all to gather together up here.

Valerie Fox Of course! He has an announcement.

De Wit Dupont-Dufort I believe he may have, yes.

Valerie Fox Of course.

Marcee Dupont-Dufort Really. Tell me, De Wit. What would you be celebrating?

Gene bounds in with the Small Boy and Uncle Job. Uncle Job is dressed identically to the Small Boy. For flying.

Valerie Fox Jack. You're here. We're here. All. You see?

Gene Yes. I'm so sorry to have kept you all waiting. It was a little tricky to get up here without being detected from the pool house.

Mrs Fox All those positively awful –

Gene You may remember Mr Job English and his ward, the young Mr Madensale?

Mrs Fox Oh! Yes of course. There are so many of you down there, aren't there?

Uncle Job We're surely grateful that you let us land our little crop-duster in your front yard.

Mrs Fox It's you with the airplane?

Uncle Job That's right. Soon as we heard that this fella here had been found we hot-footed it over.

Mrs Fox Over from?

Uncle Job California.

Marcee Dupont-Dufort (*badly disguised*) Oh! The Californians.

De Wit Dupont-Dufort Nothing wrong with California, Marcee.

Marcee Dupont-Dufort California is perfectly fine for sun or the making of movies, but it's not exactly the kinda place you look to for, well – I'm sure you understand, Mr English – pedigree of the kind we're speaking of here with Captain Fox.

Uncle Job You'll have to excuse me, ma'am. I only just about understood one half of what you just said. I heard 'California' and 'sun' and then it sounded like you were talking about dogs.

Marcee Dupont-Dufort Dogs?

De Wit Dupont-Dufort 'Pedigree', Marcee.

James comes in with a pitcher of drinks.

James You wanted drinks up here, sir?

De Wit Dupont-Dufort Attaboy.

Valerie Fox Jack. Mr Dupont-Dufort said that you wanted to speak to us.

Gene Yes.

James *(to Uncle Job)* Can I get you anything, sir?

Uncle Job No thanks. I never touch a drop when I'm flying. *(Referring to the Small Boy.)* But he'll take a glass of milk. Poor little fella's been surviving on beef jerky and cold potato salad the last twenty-four hours.

James I'll be right back.

He goes.

Valerie Fox Well, Jack, if you have something to share, here we are.

George Fox We certainly are.

Valerie Fox George, you're being supercilious.

George Fox I try.

Valerie Fox (*to Gene*) So?

Gene Of course. I'm sorry to have kept you all waiting, but I have an announcement to make.

Valerie Fox At last.

Gene I've been chatting with Uncle Job here –

Valerie Fox Uncle Job?

Mrs Fox That seems a little – over-familiar.

Gene Familiar! Yes. That's exactly what I'm trying to tell you. Determined to make sense of my murky past, as it were, I took the opportunity to have a brief chat with Uncle Job and young Mr Madensale here.

Valerie Fox Why do you keep calling this man Uncle Job?

Gene Mr English, perhaps –

Uncle Job As you may know, I am the guardian of this young gentleman here who, for years, since the tragic passing of his momma and poppa in a terrible aviation disaster in Great Bend, Kansas, has sought to discover the whereabouts of his only known relative. A long-lost nephew born twenty-six years before young Mr Madensale here to his, well, frankly over-sexed grandfather and his much younger wife.

Mrs Fox No telling the creative powers of the libido, Mr English.

Marcee Dupont-Dufort Surely, you're not suggesting –

Uncle Job I'm not suggesting anything, ma'am.

Marcee Dupont-Dufort There are many, many unaccounted for persons all over the world, and what about this particular case makes you think that –

Uncle Job There's proof!

Marcee Dupont-Dufort I beg your pardon?

De Wit Dupont-Dufort Steady, Marcee.

Valerie Fox What are you saying?

George Fox Down, Valerie.

Mrs Fox More proof than a mother's love may offer?

Uncle Job *Physical* proof.

Valerie Fox Physical?

Uncle Job A scar.

Valerie Fox (*leering at Gene*) Scar?

Uncle Job Apparently it was well known in family circles that this long-lost nephew bore a scar.

Valerie Fox And where was this scar?

Uncle Job Under his left shoulder blade.

Valerie Fox Jack, no –

Gene I do wish you'd stop calling me that, Mrs Fox.

George Fox Let the man finish, Val, for heaven's sake.

Uncle Job Apparently it's so small that it could almost go unnoticed. We just need to see that the scar does in fact exist and we'll be out of your hair, as they say in the movies.

Marcee Dupont-Dufort (*disgust*) California.

De Wit Dupont-Dufort Why don'tcha have a martini, Marcee?

Mrs Fox Are you telling me that I might have mistaken my own son, Mr English?

George Fox That's pretty much what he's saying.

Marcee Dupont-Dufort This is preposterous. Show him there's no scar there.

Gene If you insist.

Gene places himself at the centre of the room.
Everybody huddles behind him. The only one who
doesn't is the Small Boy. He remains facing Gene.

Small Boy Is it really there?

Gene begins to raise his shirt.

Gene Just wait. Two – three –

The back of his shirt is now raised to the level of his
shoulder blade. A high-pitched scream. Gene winks at
the Small Boy.
   Valerie launches herself at Gene. The rest hold her
back. The following five speeches are simultaneous:

Valerie Fox How could you? How could you do this?
What are you doing? Why are you doing this to me?

Mrs Fox (*simultaneously*) Hold her back. She's gone
mad. Please, or we shall be forced to call Dr Patchalk.

De Wit Dupont-Dufort (*simultaneously*) You may
wanna control that wife of yours.

George Fox (*simultaneously*) Val! Val! That's enough!
Enough! Do you hear me? Do you hear me? That's
enough! Enough!

Marcee Dupont-Dufort (*simultaneously*) This is so
embarrassing. To spend all this time. To come all this
way. To take all this trouble and to find out, he's a
Californian!

De Wit Dupont-Dufort Well, looks like that's that, then,
Marcee.

Marcee Dupont-Dufort Mrs Fox, I don't know what to say. I felt sure –

Mrs Fox I always doubted that this man was my son. Such a lack of real feeling can only be accounted for in the mentally impaired or a stranger.

Gene Which are you suggesting I am, Mrs Fox?

Mrs Fox A stranger, of course.

Gene Made strange perhaps by a mother who would sacrifice one son's dignity for the other's love.

Mrs Fox I'm sure I don't know what you're talking about, Mr – Mr Madensale. But, if you and your Uncle here would kindly remove your crop-dusting airplane from our lawn I'd be most appreciative. I'm assuming, Mrs Dupont-Dufort, that you will be informing the gathered crowd.

Marcee Dupont-Dufort What?

Mrs Fox Well, someone has to brave the masses in the pool house.

Marcee Dupont-Dufort The . . .

De Wit Dupont-Dufort Come on, Marcee. I'll give you a hand batting away the flying cold potato salad.

Marcee Dupont-Dufort The flying . . .

De Wit Dupont-Dufort You're not going to be popular is what I'm saying.

Marcee Dupont-Dufort What do you mean? De Wit? What does that mean?

James arrives with the milk.

James Milk!

Mrs Fox Give the child the milk, will you?

He does.

Uncle Job You drink up. We got a long flight ahead.

Gene I should bid my farewells.

Mrs Fox How does one bid farewell to a stranger?

Gene By simply saying goodbye, Mrs Fox.

Mrs Fox Well. Goodbye then.

She makes her way to the door.

Gene Mrs Dupont-Dufort.

Marcee Dupont-Dufort There's a family in Saratoga Springs who are looking for a long-lost cousin. I don't suppose you'd –

Gene Goodbye and thank you. For everything.

Marcee goes to the door.

Mr. Dupont-Dufort. Good luck with the trash.

De Wit Dupont-Dufort If we're lucky we'll never lay eyes on one another again.

De Wit makes his way to the door.

Gene (*to Valerie*) Mrs Fox –

Valerie does a little faint. George catches her.

Mrs Fox Oh, Valerie. For heaven's sake!

Valerie Fox (*astonished*) George, you caught me!

George Fox Did I?

Mrs Fox Some may say letting her fall might have done a world of good.

She leaves. Followed by Marcee and De Witt. As they go . . .

Marcee Dupont-Dufort What did you mean by I'm going to have to 'bat away cold potato salad'? I haven't done anything? Have I? De Wit? What have I done?

De Wit Dupont-Dufort We got the whole drive back for that, Marcee. Lucky we carry a spare rug in the trunk. You can use that to wipe away all that egg mayonnaise.

Valerie and George go to leave.

Gene Oh! Mr Fox?

George Fox Yes?

Gene It's about your brother?

George Fox What about him?

Gene I think I know where he is.

George Fox Really?

Gene He sleeps soundly in some grave or other somewhere in France.

George Fox I see.

Gene He was just a kid, you see.

George Fox So he was.

Gene A kid you can now love without fear of ever having to clap eyes on again.

The brothers smile at one another. Valerie makes a little swoon. George catches her once again.

Valerie Fox George!

George Fox What, Val?

Valerie Fox You did it again!

George Fox What, Val?

Valerie Fox Caught me again.

George Fox Did I?

Valerie Fox It means you were –

George Fox What, Valerie?

Valerie Fox Well. Paying attention, George. I've never known you to –

George Fox Pay attention?

Valerie Fox It feels – not so bad.

George Fox Does it?

Valerie Fox To be caught like that.

George Fox Well, I suppose it feels not so bad to do the catching.

And heading out the door . . .

Valerie Fox You know that awful child of a man never meant anything to me, Georgie. You know that, don't you? It's always been you. From the very beginning . . .

The Small Boy places his finished glass of milk on James's tray.

Small Boy Thank you.

James You're welcome.

The Small Boy has the record that George discarded earlier. He is at the record player.

Uncle Job You got something warm to put on? It gets cold up there.

Gene James? You got a woolly something or other you can loan me? We Californians aren't so used to the cooler elements.

James (*at the armoire*) There should be something here.

Uncle Job I'll go get the old girl started.

He goes, almost colliding with Juliette who rushes in with coat and suitcase.

Gene Oh God. Juliette.

Juliette I'm all set.

Gene You are?

Juliette Sure am.

Gene Juliette, I hate to break it to you, but it turns out –

Juliette What?

Gene It turns out I'm not this Jack Fox fella after all.

Juliette Is that so, is it?

Gene It would appear so.

Juliette It turns out that way, does it?

Gene I'm afraid so.

Juliette I see. Well, as long as my bag's packed I might as well take the opportunity and do something I shoulda done fifteen years ago.

Gene What's that?

She slaps Gene hard on the cheek.

James What's got into you, girl?!

Juliette Some common sense is what.

And she turns and marches out of the room.

Small Boy (*putting the record on the record player*) I don't think that that lady liked you too much.

Gene Yeah? Well, maybe 'that lady' had me confused with someone who was not too likeable.

From the record player Charles Trénet sings . . .
   'Tombé du ciel'.

James Here, try this.

   He helps Gene on with a jacket and a hat. As he does:

Gene You know, James. You never did tell me what *you* made of Captain Fox.

James Take my advice, sir, and stay out of what folks make of other folks. It tells you more about the folks doing the making than the folks being made out.

Gene How did he treat you, though? Well?

James He treated me like any other man treated me.

Gene So, I can assume, not very well.

James I didn't say that.

Gene I'm sorry then.

James What about?

Gene He's sorry. We're sorry. We both are. You know what I mean.

James Thank you. Gene.

   Gene smiles.

Gene (*to the Small Boy – the jacket*) What do you think?

   The Small Boy nods his approval.

Fine. So. Take my hand, would you?

   The Small Boy gives Gene his hand.

We got a whole lifetime of catching up to do.

Small Boy California's a long way.

Gene Just as well then. Where should we begin?

Small Boy I dunno.

Gene What about pets? You got any pets?

Small Boy I got a dog called Ace.

Gene Ace! I always wanted a dog called Ace!

Small Boy Really?

Gene Sure did.

Small Boy And a couple of cats. But they don't have names.

Gene Cats, huh?

Small Boy We just call them 'the cats'.

Gene Couple of cats sounds just fine. How about food? You got a favourite food?

Small Boy I like bacon.

Gene Bacon! I think I could get to liking bacon. And bananas. What about bananas? You like bananas?

Small Boy I like bananas.

Gene You don't say! I believe I could go bananas for bananas. And Cheesy Puffs?

Both leaving the room behind.

How's about Cheesy Puffs? You like Cheesy Puffs?

James looks around for a moment. Everyone has gone. He gathers up one or two of the stuffed animals in order to take them back up to the attic. He spies the half-drunk pitcher of martinis. He puts the stuffed animals down and fixes himself a drink. He turns up the music on the portable record player. A single-engine crop-duster roars into life on the other side of the pool. James goes out on to the balcony with his martini just in time to see the airplane take off and pass overhead. The music swells as James takes a nice long drink and watches the crop-duster climb higher and higher, then bank . . .

And chase the sunset ever west.

The End.